DR. BREEN'S
PRACTICE

William Dean Howells

1st WORLD
LIBRARY
Literary Society

Dr. Breen's Practice

William Dean Howells

© 1st World Library, 2006
PO Box 2211
Fairfield, IA 52556
www.1stworldlibrary.com
First Edition

LCCN: 2006935362

Softcover ISBN: 1-4218-2507-4
Hardcover ISBN: 1-4218-2407-8
eBook ISBN: 1-4218-2607-0

Purchase *"Dr. Breen's Practice"*
as a traditional bound book at:
www.1stWorldLibrary.com/purchase.asp?ISBN=1-4218-2507-4

1ˢᵗ World Library Literary Society

Giving Back to the World

"If you want to work on the core problem, it's early school literacy."

- James Barksdale, former CEO of Netscape

"No skill is more crucial to the future of a child, or to a democratic and prosperous society, than literacy."

- Los Angeles Times

Literacy... means far more than learning how to read and write... The aim is to transmit... knowledge and promote social participation."

- UNESCO

"Literacy is not a luxury, it is a right and a responsibility. If our world is to meet the challenges of the twenty-first century we must harness the energy and creativity of all our citizens."

- President Bill Clinton

"Parents should be encouraged to read to their children, and teachers should be equipped with all available techniques for teaching literacy, so the varying needs and capacities of individual kids can be taken into account."

- Hugh Mackay

I

Near the verge of a bold promontory stands the hotel, and looks southeastward over a sweep of sea unbroken to the horizon. Behind it stretches the vast forest, which after two hundred years has resumed the sterile coast wrested from it by the first Pilgrims, and has begun to efface the evidences of the inroad made in recent years by the bold speculator for whom Jocelyn's is named. The young birches and spruces are breast high in the drives and avenues at Jocelyn's; the low blackberry vines and the sweet fern cover the carefully-graded sidewalks, and obscure the divisions of the lots; the children of the boarders have found squawberries in the public square on the spot where the band-stand was to have been. The notion of a sea-side resort at this point was courageously conceived, and to a certain extent it was generously realized. Except for its remoteness from the railroad, a drawback which future enterprise might be expected to remedy in some way, the place has many natural advantages. The broad plateau is cooled by a breeze from the vast forests behind it, which comes laden with health and freshness from the young pines; the sea at its feet is warmed by the Gulf Stream to a temperature delicious for bathing. There are certainly mosquitoes from the woods; but there are mosquitoes everywhere, and the report that people have been driven away by them is manifestly untrue, for whoever comes to Jocelyn's remains. The beach at the foot of the bluff is almost a mile at its curve, and it is so smooth and hard that it glistens like polished marble when newly washed by the tide. It is true that you reach it from the top by a flight of eighty steps, but it was intended to have an elevator, like those near the Whirlpool at Niagara. In the mean time it is easy enough to go down, and the ladies go down every day, taking their novels or their needle-work with them. They have various notions of a bath: some conceive that it is bathing to sit in the edge of the water, and emit shrieks as the surge sweeps against them; others run boldly in, and after a moment of poignant hesitation jump up and down half-a-dozen times, and run out; yet others imagine it better to remain immersed to the chin for a given space, looking toward the shore with lips tightly shut and the breath held. But after the bath they are all of one mind; they lay their shawls on the warm sand, and, spreading out their hair to dry, they doze in the sun, in such coils and masses as the unconscious figure lends itself to. When they rise from their beds, they sit in the shelter of the cliff and knit or sew, while one of them reads aloud, and another stands watch to announce the coming of the seals, which frequent a reef near the shore in great numbers. It has been said at rival points on the coast that the ladies linger there in despair of ever being able to remount to the hotel. A young man who clambered along the shore from one of those points reported finding day after day the same young lady stretched out on the same shawl, drying the same yellow hair, who had apparently never gone upstairs since the season began. But the recurrence of this phenomenon in this spot at the very moment when the young man came by might have been accounted for upon other theories. Jocelyn's was so secluded that she could not have expected any one to find her there twice, and if she had expected this she would not have permitted it. Probably he saw a different young lady each time.

Many of the same boarders come year after year, and these tremble at the suggestion of a change for the better in Jocelyn's. The landlord has always believed that Jocelyn's would come up, some day, when times got better. He believes that the narrow-gauge railroad from New Leyden - arrested on paper at the disastrous moment when the fortunes of Jocelyn's felt the general crash - will be pushed through yet; and every summer he promises that next summer they are going to have a steam-launch running twice a day from Leyden Harbor. But

William Dean Howells

at present his house is visited once a day by a barge, as the New England coast-folks call the vehicle in which they convey city boarders to and from the station, and the old frequenters of the place hope that the station will never be nearer Jocelyn's than at present. Some of them are rich enough to afford a sojourn at more fashionable resorts; but most of them are not, though they are often people of polite tastes and of aesthetic employments. They talk with slight of the large watering-places, and probably they would not like them, though it is really economy that inspires their passion for Jocelyn's with most of them, and they know of the splendid weariness of Newport mostly by hearsay. New arrivals are not favored, but there are not often new arrivals at Jocelyn's. The chief business of the barge is to bring fresh meat for the table and the gaunt bag which contains the mail; for in the first flush of the enterprise the place was made a post-office, and the landlord is postmaster; he has the help of the lady-boarders in his official duties.

Scattered about among the young birches there are several of those pine frames known as shells, within easy walk of the hotel, where their inmates board. They are picturesque inter-iors, and are on informal terms with the public as to many domestic details. The lady of the house, doing her back hair at her dressing-room glass, is divided from her husband, smoking at the parlor fire-place, only by a partition of unlathed stud-ding. The arrest of development in these shells is characteristic of everything about the place. None of the improvements invented since the hard times began have been added to Jocelyn's; lawntennis is still unknown there; but there is a croquet-ground before the hotel, where the short, tough grass is kept in tolerable order. The wickets are pretty rusty, and it is usually the children who play; but toward the close of a certain, afternoon a young lady was pushing the balls about there. She seemed to be going over a game just played, and trying to trace the cause of her failure. She made bad shots, and laughed at her blunders. Another young lady drooped languidly on a bench at the side of the croquet-ground, and followed her movements with indifference.

"I don't see how you did it, Louise," panted the player; "it's astonishing how you beat me."

The lady on the bench made as if to answer, but ended by coughing hoarsely.

"Oh, dear child!" cried the first, dropping her mallet, and running to her. "You ought to have put on your shawl!" She lifted the knit shawl lying beside her on the bench, and laid it across the other's shoulders, and drew it close about her neck.

"Oh, don't!" said the other. "It chokes me to be bundled up so tight." She shrugged the shawl down to her shoulders with a pretty petulance. "If my chest's protected, that's all that's necessary." But she made no motion to drape the outline which her neatly-fitted dress displayed, and she did not move from her place, or look up at her anxious friend.

"Oh, but don't sit here, Louise," the latter pleaded, lingering near her. "I was wrong to let you sit down at all after you had got heated."

"Well, Grace, I had to," said she who was called Louise. "I was so tired out. I'm not going to take more cold. I can always tell when I am. I'll put on the shawl in half a minute; or else I'll go in."

"I'm sure there's nothing to keep me out. That's the worst of these lonely places: my mind preys upon itself. That's what Dr. Nixon always said: he said it was no use in air so long as my mind preyed upon itself. He said that I ought to divert my mind all I could, and keep it from preying upon itself; that it was worth all the medicine in the world."

"That's perfectly true."

"Then you oughtn't to keep reminding me all the time that I'm sick. That's what starts my mind to preying upon itself; and when it gets going once I can't stop it. I ought to treat

William Dean Howells

myself just like a well person; that's what the doctor said."

The other stood looking at the speaker in frowning perplexity. She was a serious-faced girl, and now when she frowned her black brows met sternly above her gray eyes. But she controlled any impulse she had to severity, and asked gently, "Shall I send Bella to you?"

"Oh, no! I can't make society out of a child the whole time. I'll just sit here till the barge comes in. I suppose it will be as empty as a gourd, as usual." She added, with a sick and weary negligence, "I don't even know where Bella is. She's run off, somewhere."

"It's quite time she should be looked up, for tea. I'll wander out that way and look for her." She indicated the wilderness generally.

"Thanks," said Louise. She now gratefully drew her shawl up over her shoulders, and faced about on the bench so as to command an easy view of the arriving barge. The other met it on her way to the place in the woods where the children usually played, and found it as empty as her friend had foreboded. But the driver stopped his horses, and leaned out of the side of the wagon with a little package in his hand. He read the superscription, and then glanced consciously at the girl. "You're Miss Breen, ain't you?"

"Yes," she said, with lady-like sweetness and a sort of business-like alertness.

"Well," suggested the driver, "this is for Miss Grace Breen, M. D."

"For me, thank you," said the young lady. "I'm Dr. Breen." She put out her hand for the little package from the homoeopathic pharmacy in Boston; and the driver yielded it with a blush that reddened him to his hair.

"Well," he said slowly, staring at the handsome girl, who did not visibly share his embarrassment, "they told me you was the one; but I couldn't seem to get it through me. I thought it must be the old lady."

"My mother is Mrs. Breen," the young lady briefly explained, and walked rapidly away, leaving the driver stuck in the heavy sand of Sea-Glimpse Avenue.

"Why, get up!" he shouted to his horses. "Goin' to stay here all day?" He craned his neck round the side of the wagon for a sight of her. "Well, dumm 'f I don't wish I was sick! Steps along," he mused, watching the swirl and ripple of her skirt, "like - I dunno what."

With her face turned from him Dr. Breen blushed, too; she was not yet so used to her quality of physician that she could coldly bear the confusion to which her being a doctor put men. She laughed a little to herself at the helplessness of the driver, confronted probably for the first time with a graduate of the New York homoeopathic school; but she believed that she had reasons for taking herself seriously in every way, and she had not entered upon this career without definite purposes. When she was not yet out of her teens, she had an unhappy love affair, which was always darkly referred to as a disappointment by people who knew of it at the time. Though the particulars of the case do not directly concern this story, it may be stated that the recreant lover afterwards married her dearest girl-friend, whom he had first met in her company. It was cruel enough, and the hurt went deep; but it neither crushed nor hardened her. It benumbed her for a time; she sank out of sight; but when she returned to the knowledge of the world she showed no mark of the blow except what was thought a strange eccentricity in a girl such as she had been. The world which had known her - it was that of an inland New England city - heard of her definitely after several years as a student of medicine in New York. Those who had more of her intimacy understood that she had chosen this work with the intention of giving her life to it, in the spirit in which other

William Dean Howells

women enter convents, or go out to heathen lands; but probably this conception had its exaggerations. What was certain was that she was rich enough to have no need of her profession as a means of support, and that its study had cost her more than the usual suffering that it brings to persons of sensitive nerves. Some details were almost insuperably repugnant; but in schooling herself to them she believed that she was preparing to encounter anything in the application of her science.

Her first intention had been to go back to her own town after her graduation, and begin the practice of her profession among those who had always known her, and whose scrutiny and criticism would be hardest to bear, and therefore, as she fancied, the most useful to her in the formation of character. But afterwards she relinquished her purpose in favor of a design which she thought would be more useful to others: she planned going to one of the great factory towns, and beginning practice there, in company with an older physician, among the children of the operatives. Pending the completion of this arrangement, which was waiting upon the decision of the other lady, she had come to Jocelyn's with her mother, and with Mrs. Maynard, who had arrived from the West, aimlessly sick and unfriended, just as they were about leaving home. There was no resource but to invite her with them, and Dr. Breen was finding her first patient in this unexpected guest. She did not wholly regret the accident; this, too, was useful work, though not that she would have chosen; but her mother, after a fortnight, openly repined, and could not mention Mrs. Maynard without some rebellious murmur. She was an old lady, who had once kept a very vigilant conscience for herself; but after making her life unhappy with it for some threescore years, she now applied it entirely to the exasperation and condemnation of others. She especially devoted it to fretting a New England girl's naturally morbid sense of duty in her daughter, and keeping it in the irritation of perpetual self-question. She had never actively opposed her studying medicine; that ambition had harmonized very well with certain radical tendencies of her own, and it was at least not marriage, which she had found tolerable only in its modified form of widowhood; but at every step after the decisive step was taken she was beset with misgivings lest Grace was not fully alive to the grave responsibilities of her office, which she accumulated upon the girl in proportion as she flung off all responsibilities of her own. She was doubtless deceived by that show of calm which sometimes deceived Grace herself, who, in tutoring her soul to bear what it had to bear, mistook her tense effort for spiritual repose, and scarcely realized through her tingling nerves the strain she was undergoing. In spite of the bitter experience of her life, she was still very ardent in her hopes of usefulness, very scornful of distress or discomfort to herself, and a little inclined to exact the heroism she was ready to show. She had a child's severe morality, and she had hardly learned to understand that there is much evil in the world that does not characterize the perpetrators: she held herself as strictly to account for every word and deed as she held others, and she had an almost passionate desire to meet the consequence of her errors; till that was felt, an intolerable doom hung over her. She tried not to be impulsive; that was criminal in one of her calling; and she struggled for patience with an endeavor that was largely successful.

As to the effect of her career outside of herself, and of those whom her skill was to benefit, she tried to think neither arrogantly nor meanly. She would not entertain the vanity that she was serving what is called the cause of woman, and she would not assume any duties or responsibilities toward it. She thought men were as good as women; at least one man had been no worse than one woman; and it was in no representative or exemplary character that she had chosen her course. At the same time that she held these sane opinions, she believed that she had put away the hopes with the pleasures that might once have taken her as a young girl. In regard to what had changed the current of her life, she mentally asserted her mere nullity, her absolute non-existence. The thought of it no longer rankled, and that interest could never be hers again. If it had not been so much like affectation, and so counter to her strong aesthetic instinct, she might have made her dress

William Dean Howells

somehow significant of her complete abeyance in such matters; but as it was she only studied simplicity, and as we have seen from the impression of the barge-driver she did not finally escape distinction in dress and manner. In fact, she could not have escaped that effect if she would; and it was one of the indomitable contradictions of her nature that she would not.

When she came back to the croquet-ground, leading the little girl by the hand, she found Mrs. Maynard no longer alone and no longer sad. She was chatting and laughing with a slim young fellow, whose gay blue eyes looked out of a sunburnt face, and whose straw hat, carried in his hand, exposed a closely shaven head. He wore a suit of gray flannel, and Mrs. Maynard explained that he was camping on the beach at Birkman's Cove, and had come over in the steamer with her when she returned from Europe. She introduced him as Mr. Libby, and said, "Oh, Bella, you dirty little thing!"

Mr. Libby bowed anxiously to Grace, and turned for refuge to the little girl. "Hello, Bella!" "Hello!" said the child. "Remember me?" The child put her left hand on that of Grace holding her right, and prettily pressed her head against the girl's arm in bashful silence. Grace said some coldly civil words to the young man: without looking at Mrs. Maynard, and passed on into the house.

"You don't mean that's your doctor?" he scarcely more than whispered.

"Yes, I do," answered Mrs. Maynard. "Isn't she too lovely? And she's just as good! She used to stand up at school for me, when all the girls were down on me because I was Western. And when I came East, this time, I just went right straight to her house. I knew she could tell me exactly what to do. And that's the reason I'm here. I shall always recommend this air to anybody with lung difficulties. It's the greatest thing! I'm almost another person. Oh, you needn't look after her, Mr. Libby! There's nothing flirtatious about Grace," said Mrs. Maynard.

The young man recovered himself from his absentminded stare in the direction Grace had taken, with a frank laugh. "So much the better for a fellow, I should say!"

Grace handed the little girl over to her nurse, and went to her own room, where she found her mother waiting to go down to tea.

"Where is Mrs. Maynard?" asked Mrs. Breen.

"Out on the croquet-ground," answered the daughter.

"I should think it would be damp," suggested Mrs. Green.

"She will come in when the tea-bell rings. She wouldn't come in now, if I told her."

"Well," said the elder lady, "for a person who lets her doctor pay her board, I think 'she's very independent."

"I wish you wouldn't speak of that, mother," said the girl.

"I can't help it, Grace. It's ridiculous, - that's what it is; it's ridiculous."

"I don't see anything ridiculous in it. A physician need not charge anything unless he chooses, or she; and if I choose to make Louise my guest here it's quite the same as if she were my guest at home."

"I don't like you to have such a guest," said Mrs. Green. "I don't see what claim she has upon your hospitality."

"She has a double claim upon it," Grace answered, with a flush. "She is in sickness and in trouble. I don't see how she could have a better claim. Even if she were quite well I should consider the way she had been treated by her husband sufficient, and I should want to do everything I could for her."

William Dean Howells

"I should want her to behave herself," said Mrs. Breen dryly.

"How behave herself? What do you mean?" demanded Grace, with guilty heat.

"You know what I mean, Grace. A woman in her position ought to be more circumspect than any other woman, if she wants people to believe that her husband treated her badly."

"We oughtn't to blame her for trying to forget her troubles. It's essential to her recovery for her to be as cheerful as she can be. I know that she's impulsive, and she's free in her manners with strangers; but I suppose that's her Westernism. She's almost distracted. She was crying half the night, with her troubles, and kept Bella and me both awake."

"Is Bella with her now?"

"No," Grace admitted. "Jane's getting her ready to go down with us. Louise is talking with a gentleman who came over on the steamer with her; he's camping on the beach near here. I didn't wait to hear particulars."

When the nurse brought the little girl to their door, Mrs. Green took one hand and Grace the other, and they led her down to tea. Mrs. Maynard was already at table, and told them all about meeting Mr. Libby abroad.

Until the present time she and Grace had not seen each other since they were at school together in Southington, where the girl used to hear so much to the disadvantage of her native section that she would hardly have owned to it if her accent had not found her out. It would have been pleasanter to befriend another person, but the little Westerner suffered a veritable persecution, and that was enough to make Grace her friend. Shortly after she returned home from school she married, in that casual and tentative fashion in which so many marriages seem made. Grace had heard of her as travelling in Europe with her husband, from whom she was now separated.

She reported that he had known Mr. Libby in his bachelor days, and that Mr. Libby had travelled with them. Mr. Maynard appeared to have left to Mr. Libby the arrangement of his wife's pleasures, the supervision of her shopping, and the direction of their common journeys and sojourns; and it seemed to have been indifferent to him whether his friend was smoking and telling stories with him, or going with his wife to the opera, or upon such excursions as he had no taste for. She gave the details of the triangular intimacy with a frank unconsciousness; and after nine o'clock she returned from a moonlight walk on the beach with Mr. Libby.

Grace sat waiting for her at the little one's bedside, for Bella had been afraid to go to sleep alone.

"How good you are!" cried Louise, in a grateful under-tone, as she came in. She kissed Grace, and choked down a cough with her hand over her mouth.

"Louise," said Grace sternly, "this is shameful! You forget that you are married, and ill, too."

"Oh, I'm ever so much better, to-night. The air's just as dry! And you needn't mind Mr. Libby. He's such an old friend! Besides, I'm sure to gain the case."

"No matter. Even as a divorced woman, you oughtn't to go on in this way."

"Well, I wouldn't, with every one. But it's quite different with Mr. Libby. And, besides, I have to keep my mind from preying on itself somehow."

William Dean Howells

II

Mrs. Maynard sat in the sun on the seaward-looking piazza of the hotel, and coughed in the warm air. She told the ladies, as they came out from breakfast, that she was ever so much better generally, but that she seemed to have more of that tickling in her throat. Each of them advised her for good, and suggested this specific and that; and they all asked her what Miss Breen was doing for her cough. Mrs. Maynard replied, between the paroxysms, that she did not know: it was some kind of powders. Then they said they would think she would want to try something active; even those among them who were homoeopathists insinuated a fine distrust of a physician of their own sex. "Oh, it's nothing serious," Mrs. Maynard explained. "It's just bronchial. The air will do me more good than anything. I'm keeping out in it all I can."

After they were gone, a queer, gaunt man came and glanced from the doorway at her. He had one eye in unnatural fixity, and the other set at that abnormal slant which is said to qualify the owner for looking round a corner before he gets to it. A droll twist of his mouth seemed partly physical, but: there is no doubt that he had often a humorous intention.

It was Barlow, the man-of-all-work, who killed and plucked the poultry, peeled the potatoes and picked the peas, pulled the sweet-corn and the tomatoes, kindled the kitchen fire, harnessed the old splayfooted mare, - safe for ladies and children, and intolerable for all others, which formed the entire stud of the Jocelyn House stables, - dug the clams, rowed and sailed the boat, looked after the bath-houses, and came in contact with the guests at so many points that he was on easy terms with them all. This ease tended to an intimacy which he was himself powerless to repress, and which, from time to time, required their intervention. He now wore a simple costume of shirt and trousers, the latter terminated by a pair of broken shoes, and sustained by what he called a single gallows; his broad-brimmed straw hat scooped down upon his shoulders behind, and in front added to his congenital difficulty of getting people in focus. "How do you do, this morning, Mrs. Maynard?" he said.

"Oh, I'm first-rate, Mr. Barlow. What sort of day do you think it's going to be for a sail?"

Barlow came out to the edge of the piazza, and looked at the sea and sky. "First-rate. Fog's most burnt away now. You don't often see a fog at Jocelyn's after ten o'clock in the mornin'."

He looked for approval to Mrs. Maynard, who said, "That's so. The air's just splendid. It's doing everything for me."

"It's these pine woods, back o' here. Every breath on 'em does ye good. It's the balsam in it. D' you ever try," he asked, stretching his hand as far up the piazza-post as he could, and swinging into a conversational posture, - "d' you ever try whiskey - good odd Bourbon whiskey - with white-pine chips in it?"

Mrs. Maynard looked up with interest, but, shaking her head, coughed for no.

"Well, I should like to have you try that."

"What does it do?" she gasped, when she could get her breath.

"Well, it's soothin' t' the cough, and it builds ye up, every ways. Why, my brother," continued the factotum, "he died of consumption when I was a boy, - reg'lar old New England consumption. Don't hardly ever hear of it any more, round here. Well, I don't suppose there's been a case of reg'lar old New England consumption - well, not the old New England kind - since these woods growed up. He used to take whiskey with white-pine chips in it; and I can remember hearin 'em say that it done him more good than all the doctor's stuff. He'd been out to Demarary, and everywheres, and he come home in the last stages, and took up with this whiskey with whitepine chips in it. Well, it's just like this, I presume it's the balsam in the chips. It don't make any difference how you git the balsam into your system, so's 't you git it there. I should like to have you try whiskey with white-pine chips in it."

He looked convincingly at Mrs. Maynard, who said she should like to try it. "It's just bronchial with me, you know. But I should like to try it. I know it would be soothing; and I've always heard that whiskey was the very thing to build you up. But," she added, lapsing from this vision of recovery, "I couldn't take it unless Grace said so. She'd be sure to find it out."

"Why, look here," said Barlow. "As far forth as that goes, you could keep the bottle in my room. Not but what I believe in going by your doctor's directions, it don't matter who your doctor is. I ain't sayin' nothin' against Miss Breen, you understand?"

"Oh, no!" cried Mrs. Maynard.

"I never see much nicer ladies than her and her mother in the house. But you just tell her about the whiskey with the white-pine chips in it. Maybe she never heard of it. Well, she hain't had a great deal of experience yet."

"No," said Mrs. Maynard. "And I think she'll be glad to hear of it. You may be sure I'll tell her, Mr. Barlow. Grace is everything for the balsamic properties of the air, down here. That's what she said; and as you say, it doesn't matter how you get the balsam into your system, so you get it there."

"No," said the factotum, in a tone of misgiving, as if the repetition of the words presented the theory in a new light to him.

"What I think is, and what I'm always telling Grace," pursued Mrs. Maynard, in that confidential spirit in which she helplessly spoke of her friends by their first names to every one, "that if I could once get my digestion all right, then the cough would stop of itself. The doctor said - Dr. Nixon, that is - that it was more than half the digestion any way. But just as soon as I eat anything - or if I over-eat a little - then that tickling in my throat begins, and then I commence coughing; and I'm back just where I was. It's the digestion. I oughtn't to have eaten that mince pie, yesterday."

"No," admitted Barlow. Then he said, in indirect defence of the kitchen, "I think you hadn't ought to be out in the night air, - well, not a great deal."

"Well, I don't suppose it does do me much good," Mrs. Maynard said, turning her eyes seaward.

Barlow let his hand drop from the piazza post, and slouched in-doors; but he came out again as if pricked by conscience to return.

"After all, you know, it didn't cure him."

"What cure him?" asked Mrs. Maynard.

"The whiskey with the white-pine chips in it."

"Cure who?"

"My brother."

"Oh! Oh, yes! But mine's only bronchial. I think it might do me good. I shall tell Grace about it."

Barlow looked troubled, as if his success in the suggestion of this remedy were not finally a pleasure; but as Mrs. Maynard kept her eyes persistently turned from him, and was evidently tired, he had nothing for it but to go in-doors again. He met Grace, and made way for her on the threshold to pass out.

As she joined Mrs. Maynard, "Well, Grace," said the latter, "I do believe you are right. I have taken some more cold. But that shows that it doesn't get worse of itself, and I think we ought to be encouraged by that. I'm going to be more careful of the night air after this."

"I don't think the night air was the worst thing about it, Louise," said Grace bluntly.

"You mean the damp from the sand? I put on my rubbers."

"I don't mean the damp sand," said Grace, beginning to pull over some sewing which she had in her lap, and looking down at it.

Mrs. Maynard watched her a while in expectation that she would say more, but she did not speak. "Oh - well!" she was forced to continue herself, "if you're going to go on with that!"

"The question is," said Grace, getting the thread she wanted, "whether you are going on with it."

"Why, I can't see any possible harm in it," protested Mrs. Maynard. "I suppose you don't exactly like my going with Mr. Libby, and I know that under some circumstances it wouldn't be quite the thing. But didn't I tell you last night how he lived with us in Europe? And when we were all coming over on the steamer together Mr. Libby and Mr. Maynard were together the whole time, smoking and telling stories. They were the greatest friends! Why, it isn't as if he was a stranger, or an enemy of Mr. Maynard's."

Grace dropped her sewing into her lap. "Really, Louise, you're incredible!" She looked sternly at the invalid; but broke into a laugh, on which Mrs. Maynard waited with a puzzled face. As Grace said nothing more, she helplessly resumed: -

"We didn't expect to go down the cliff when he first called in the evening. But he said he would help me up again, and - he did, nicely. I wasn't exhausted a bit; and how I took more cold I can't understand; I was wrapped up warmly. I think I took the cold when I was sitting there after our game of croquet, with my shawl off. Don't you think so?" she wheedled.

"Perhaps," said Grace.

"He did nothing but talk about you, Grace," said Mrs. Maynard, with a sly look at the other. "He's awfully afraid of you, and he kept asking about you."

"Louise," said the other, gravely ignoring these facts, "I never undertook the care of you socially, and I object very much to lecturing you. You are nearly as old as I am, and you have had a great deal more experience of life than I have." Mrs. Maynard sighed deeply in assent. "But it doesn't seem to have taught you that if you will provoke people to talk of you, you must expect criticism. One after another you've told nearly every woman in the house your affairs, and they have all sympathized with you and pitied you. I shall have to be plain, and tell you that I can't have them sneering and laughing at any one who is my guest. I can't let you defy public opinion here."

"Why, Grace," said Mrs. Maynard, buoyed above offence at her friend's words by her consciousness of the point she was about to make, "you defy public opinion yourself a good deal more than I do, every minute."

"I? How do I defy it?" demanded Grace indignantly.

"By being a doctor."

Grace opened her lips to speak, but she was not a ready person, and she felt the thrust. Before she could say anything Mrs. Maynard went on: "There isn't one of them that doesn't think you're much more scandalous than if you were the greatest flirt alive. But, I don't mind them, and why should you?"

The serious girl whom she addressed was in that helpless subjection to the truth in which so many New England women pass their lives. She could not deny the truth which lurked in the exaggeration of these words, and it unnerved her, as the fact that she was doing what the vast majority of women considered unwomanly always unnerved her when she suffered herself to think of it. "You are right, Louise," she said meekly and sadly. "They think as well of you as they do of me."

"Yes, that's just what I said!" cried Mrs. Maynard, glad of her successful argument.

But however disabled, her friend resumed: "The only safe way for you is to take the ground that so long as you wear your husband's name you must honor it, no matter how cruel and indifferent to you he has been."

"Yes," assented Mrs. Maynard ruefully, "of course."

"I mean that you mustn't even have the appearance of liking admiration, or what you call attentions. It's wicked."

"I suppose so," murmured the culprit.

"You have been brought up to have such different ideas of divorce from what I have," continued Grace, "that I don't feel as if I had any right to advise you about what you are to do after you gain your suit."

"I shall not want to get married again for one while; I know that much," Mrs. Maynard interpolated self-righteously.

"But till you do gain it, you ought not to regard it as

emancipating you in the slightest degree."

"No," came in sad assent from the victim of the law's delays.

"And I want you to promise me that you won't go walking with Mr. Libby any more; and that you won't even see him alone, after this."

"Why, but Grace!" cried Mrs. Maynard, as much in amazement as in annoyance. "You don't seem to understand! Haven't I told you he was a friend of the family? He's quite as much Mr. Maynard's friend as he is mine. I'm sure," she added, "if I asked Mr. Libby, I should never think of getting divorced. He's all for George; and it's as much as I can do to put up with him."

"No matter. That doesn't alter the appearance to people here. I don't wish you to go with him alone any more."

"Well, Grace, I won't," said Mrs. Maynard earnestly. "I won't, indeed. And that makes me think: he wanted you to go along this morning."

"To go along? Wanted me - What are you talking about?"

"Why, I suppose that's his boat, out there, now." Mrs. Maynard pointed to a little craft just coming to anchor inside the reef. "He said he wanted me to take a sail with him, this morning; and he said he would come up and ask you, too. I do hope you'll go, Grace. It's just as calm; and he always has a man with him to help sail the boat, so there isn't the least danger." Grace looked at her in silent sorrow, and Mrs. Maynard went on with sympathetic seriousness: "Oh! there's one thing I want to ask you about, Grace: I don't like to have any concealments from you." Grace did not speak, but she permitted Mrs. Maynard to proceed: "Barlow recommended it, and he's lived here a great while. His brother took it, and he had the regular old New England consumption. I thought I shouldn't like to try it without your knowing it."

"Try it? What are you talking about, Louise?"

"Why, whiskey with white-pine chips in it."

Grace rose, and moved towards the door, with the things dropping from her lap. One of these was a spool, that rolled down the steps and out upon the sandy road. She turned to pursue it, and recovered it at the cost of dropping her scissors and thimble out of opposite sides of her skirt, which she had gathered up apronwise to hold her work. When she rose from the complicated difficulty, in which Mrs. Maynard had amiably lent her aid, she confronted Mr. Libby, who was coming towards them from the cliff. She gave him a stiff nod, and attempted to move away; but in turning round and about she had spun herself into the folds of a stout linen thread escaping from its spool. These gyves not only bound her skirts but involved her feet in an extraordinary mesh, which tightened at the first step and brought her to a standstill.

Mrs. Maynard began to laugh and cough, as Mr. Libby came to her friend's help. He got the spool in his hand, and walked around her in the endeavor to free her; but in vain. She extended him the scissors with the stern passivity of a fate. "Cut it," she commanded, and Mr. Libby knelt before her and obeyed. "Thanks," she said, taking back the scissors; and now she sat down again, and began deliberately to put up her work in her handkerchief.

"I'll go out and get my things. I won't be gone half a minute, Mr. Libby," said Mrs. Maynard, with her first breath, as she vanished indoors.

Mr. Libby leaned against the post lately occupied by the factotum in his talk with Mrs. Maynard, and looked down at Grace as she bent over her work. If he wished to speak to her, and was wavering as to the appropriate style of address for a handsome girl, who was at once a young lady and a physician, she spared him the agony of a decision by looking up at him suddenly.

"I hope," he faltered, "that you feel like a sail, this morning? Did Mrs. Maynard - "

"I shall have to excuse myself," answered Grace, with a conscience against saying she was sorry. "I am a very bad sailor."

"Well, so am I, for that matter," said Mr. Libby. "But it's smooth as a pond, to-day."

Grace made no direct response, and he grew visibly uncomfortable under the cold abstraction of the gaze with which she seemed to look through him. "Mrs. Maynard tells me you came over with her from Europe."

"Oh yes!" cried the young man, the light of pleasant recollection kindling in his gay eyes. "We had a good time. Maynard was along: he's a first-rate fellow. I wish he were here."

"Yes," said Grace, "I wish so, too." She did not know what to make of this frankness of the young man's, and she did not know whether to consider him very depraved or very innocent. In her question she continued to stare at him, without being aware of the embarrassment to which she was putting him.

"I heard of Mrs. Maynard's being here, and I thought I should find him, too. I came over yesterday to get him to go into the woods with us."

Grace decided that this was mere effrontery. "It is a pity that he is not here," she said; and though it ought to have been possible for her to go on and rebuke the young fellow for bestowing upon Mrs. Maynard the comradeship intended for her husband, it was not so. She could only look severely at him, and trust that he might conceive the intention which she could not express. She rebelled against the convention and against her own weakness, which would not let her boldly interfere in what she believed a wrong; she had defied society,

William Dean Howells

in the mass, but here, with this man, whom as an atom of the mass she would have despised, she was powerless.

"Have you ever seen him?" Libby asked, perhaps clinging to Maynard because he was a topic of conversation in default of which there might be nothing to say.

"No," answered Grace.

"He's funny. He's got lots of that Western humor, and he tells a story better than any man I ever saw. There was one story of his" -

"I have no sense of humor," interrupted Grace impatiently. "Mr. Libby," she broke out, "I 'm sorry that you've asked Mrs. Maynard to take a sail with you. The sea air" - she reddened with the shame of not being able to proceed without this wretched subterfuge - "won't do her any good."

"Then," said the young man, "you mustn't let her go."

"I don't choose to forbid her," Grace began.

"I beg your pardon," he broke in. "I'll be back in a moment."

He turned, and ran to the edge of the cliff, over which he vanished, and he did not reappear till Mrs. Maynard had rejoined Grace on the piazza.

"I hope you won't mind its being a little rough, Mrs. Maynard," he said, breathing quickly. "Adams thinks we're going to have it pretty fresh before we get back."

"Indeed, I don't want to go, then!" cried Mrs. Maynard, in petulant disappointment, letting her wraps fall upon a chair.

Mr. Libby looked at Grace, who haughtily rejected a part in the conspiracy. "I wish you to go, Louise," she declared indignantly. "I will take the risk of all the harm that comes to you from the bad weather." She picked up the shawls, and handed them to Mr. Libby, on whom her eyes blazed their contempt and wonder. It cost a great deal of persuasion and insistence now to make Mrs. Maynard go, and he left all this to Grace, not uttering a word till he gave Mrs. Maynard his hand to help her down the steps. Then he said, "Well, I wonder what Miss Breen does want."

"I 'm sure I don't know," said the other. "At first she didn't want me to go, this morning, and now she makes me. I do hope it isn't going to be a storm."

"I don't believe it is. A little fresh, perhaps. I thought you might be seasick."

"Don't you remember? I'm never seasick! That's one of the worst signs."

"Oh, yes."

"If I could be thoroughly seasick once, it would be the best thing I could do."

"Is she capricious?" asked Mr. Libby.

"Grace?" cried Mrs. Maynard, releasing her hand half-way down the steps, in order to enjoy her astonishment without limitation of any sort. "Grace capricious!"

"Yes," said Mr. Libby, "that's what I thought. Better take my hand again," and he secured that of Mrs. Maynard, who continued her descent. "I suppose I don't understand her exactly. Perhaps she didn't like my not calling her Doctor. I didn't call her anything. I suppose she thought I was dodging it. I was. I should have had to call her Miss Breen, if I called her anything."

"She wouldn't have cared. She isn't a doctor for the name of it."

"I suppose you think it's a pity?" he asked.

"What?"

"Her being a doctor."

"I'll tell her you say so."

"No, don't. But don't you?"

"Well, I wouldn't want to be one," said Mrs. Mayward candidly.

"I suppose it's all right, if she does it from a sense of duty, as you say," he suggested.

"Oh, yes, she's all right. And she's just as much of a girl as anybody; though she don't know it," Mrs. Maynard added astutely. "Why wouldn't she come with us? Were you afraid to ask her?"

"She said she wasn't a good sailor. Perhaps she thought we were too young. She must be older than you."

"Yes, and you, too!" cried Mrs. Maynard, with good-natured derision.

"She doesn't look old," returned Mr. Libby.

"She's twenty-eight. How old are you?"

"I promised the census-taker not to tell till his report came out."

"What is the color of her hair?"

"Brown."

"And her eyes?"

"I don't know!"

"You had better look out, Mr. Libby!" said Mrs. Maynard, putting her foot on the ground at last.

They walked across the beach to where his dory lay, and Grace saw him pulling out to the sail boat before she went in from the piazza. Then she went to her mother's room. The elderly lady was keeping indoors, upon a theory that the dew was on, and that it was not wholesome to go out till it was off. She asked, according to her habit when she met her daughter alone, "Where is Mrs. Maynard?"

"Why do you always ask that, mother?" retorted Grace, with her growing irritation in regard to her patient intensified by the recent interview. "I can't be with her the whole time."

"I wish you could," said Mrs. Breen, with noncommittal suggestion.

Grace could not keep herself from demanding, "Why?" as her mother expected, though she knew why too well.

"Because she wouldn't be in mischief then," returned Mrs. Breen.

"She's in mischief now!" cried the girl vehemently; "and it's my fault! I did it. I sent her off to sail with that ridiculous Mr. Libby!"

"Why?" asked Mrs. Breen, in her turn, with unbroken tranquillity.

"Because I am a fool, and I couldn't help him lie out of his engagement with her."

"Didn't he want to go?"

"I don't know. Yes. They both wanted me to go with them.

Simpletons! And while she had gone up-stairs for her wraps I managed to make him understand that I didn't wish her to go, either; and he ran down to his boat, and came back with a story about its going to be rough, and looked at me perfectly delighted, as if I should be pleased. Of course, then, I made him take her."

"And isn't it going to be rough?" asked Mrs. Green.

"Why, mother, the sea's like glass."

Mrs. Breen turned the subject. "You would have done better, Grace, to begin as you had planned. Your going to Fall River, and beginning practice there among those factory children, was the only thing that I ever entirely liked in your taking up medicine. There was sense in that. You had studied specially for it. You could have done good there."

"Oh, yes," sighed the girl, "I know. But what was I to do, when she came to us, sick and poor? I couldn't turn my back on her, especially after always befriending her, as I used to, at school, and getting her to depend on me."

"I don't see how you ever liked her," said Mrs. Breen.

"I never did like her. I pitied her. I always thought her a poor, flimsy little thing. But that oughtn't to make any difference, if she was in trouble."

"No," Mrs. Breen conceded, and in compensation Grace admitted something more on her side: "She's worse than she used to be, - sillier. I don't suppose she has a wrong thought; but she's as light as foam."

"Oh, it isn't the wicked people who, do the harm," said Mrs. Green.

"I was sure that this air would be everything for her; and so it would, with any ordinary case. But a child would take better care of itself. I have to watch her every minute, like a child; and I never know what she will do next."

"Yes; it's a burden," said Mrs. Breen, with a sympathy which she had not expressed before. "And you're a good girl, Grace," she added in very unwonted recognition.

The grateful tears stole into the daughter's eyes, but she kept a firm face, even after they began to follow one another down her cheeks. "And if Louise hadn't come, you know, mother, that I was anxious to have some older person with me when I went to Fall River. I was glad to have this respite; it gives me a chance to think. I felt a little timid about beginning alone."

"A man wouldn't," Mrs. Breen remarked.

"No. I am not a man. I have accepted that; with all the rest. I don't rebel against being a woman. If I had been a man, I shouldn't have studied medicine. You know that. I wished to be a physician because I was a woman, and because - because - I had failed where - other women's hopes are." She said it out firmly, and her mother softened to her in proportion to the girl's own strength. "I might have been just a nurse. You know I should have been willing to be that, but I thought I could be something more. But it's no use talking." She added, after an interval, in which her mother rocked to and fro with a gentle motion that searched the joints of her chair, and brought out its most plaintive squeak in pathetic iteration, and watched Grace, as she sat looking seaward through the open window, "I think it's rather hard, mother, that you should be always talking as if I wished to take my calling mannishly. All that I intend is not to take it womanishly; but as for not being a woman about it, or about anything, that's simply impossible. A woman is reminded of her insufficiency to herself every hour of the day. And it's always a man that comes to her help. I dropped some things out of my lap down there, and by the time I had gathered them up I was wound round and round with linen thread so that I couldn't move a step, and Mr. Libby cut me loose. I could have done it myself, but it seemed

William Dean Howells

right and natural that he should do it. I dare say he plumed himself upon his service to me, - that would be natural, too. I have things enough to keep me meek, mother!"

She did not look round at Mrs. Breen, who said, "I think you are morbid about it."

"Yes. And I have the satisfaction of knowing that whatever people think of Louise's giddiness, I'm, a great deal more scandalous to them than she is simply because I wish to do some good in the world, in a way that women haven't done it, usually."

"Now you are morbid."

"Oh, yes! Talk about men being obstacles! It's other women! There isn't a woman in the house that wouldn't sooner trust herself in the hands of the stupidest boy that got his diploma with me than she would in mine. Louise knows it, and she feels that she has a claim upon me in being my patient. And I've no influence with her about her conduct because she understands perfectly well that they all consider me much worse. She prides herself on doing me justice. She patronizes me. She tells me that I'm just as nice as, if I hadn't 'been through all that.'" Grace rose, and a laugh, which was half a sob, broke from her.

Mrs. Breen could not feel the humor of the predicament. "She puts you in a false position."

"I must go and see where that poor little wretch of a child is," said Grace, going out of the room. She returned in an hour, and asked her mother for the arnica. "Bella has had a bump," she explained.

"Why, have you been all this time looking for her?

"No, I couldn't find her, and I've been reading. Barlow has just brought her in. HE could find her. She fell out of a tree, and she's frightfully bruised."

She was making search on a closet shelf as she talked. When she reappeared with the bottle in her hand, her mother asked, "Isn't it very hot and close?"

"Very," said Grace.

"I should certainly think they would perish," said Mrs. Breen, hazarding the pronoun, with a woman's confidence that her interlocutor would apply it correctly.

When Grace had seen Bella properly bathed and brown-papered, and in the way to forgetfulness of her wounds in sleep, she came down to the piazza, and stood looking out to sea. The ladies appeared one by one over the edge of the cliff, and came up, languidly stringing their shawls after them, or clasping their novels to their bosoms.

"There isn't a breath down there," they said, one after another. The last one added, "Barlow says it's the hottest day he's ever seen here."

In a minute Barlow himself appeared at the head of the steps with the ladies' remaining wraps, and confirmed their report in person. "I tell you," he said, wiping his forehead, "it's a ripper."

"It must be an awful day in town," said one of the ladies, fanning herself with a newspaper.

"Is that to-day's Advertiser, Mrs. Alger?" asked another.

"Oh, dear, no! yesterday's. We sha'n't have today's till this afternoon. It shows what a new arrival you are, Mrs. Scott - your asking."

"To be sure. But it's such a comfort being where you can see the Advertiser the same morning. I always look at the Weather

William Dean Howells

Report the first thing. I like to know what the weather is going to be."

"You can't at Jocelyn's. You can only know what it's been."

"Well," Barlow interposed, jealous for Jocelyn's, "you can most al'ays tell by the look o' things."

"Yes," said one of the ladies; "but I'd rather trust the Weather Report. It's wonderful how it comes true. I don't think there's anything that you miss more in Europe than our American Weather Report."

"I'm sure you miss the oysters," said another.

"Yes," the first admitted, "you do miss the oysters. It was the last of the R months when we landed in New York; and do you know what we did the first thing - ? We drove to Fulton Market, and had one of those Fulton Market broils! My husband said we should have had it if it had been July. He used to dream of the American oysters when we were in Europe. Gentlemen are so fond of them."

Barlow, from scanning the heavens, turned round and faced the company, which had drooped in several attitudes of exhaustion on the benching of the piazza. "Well, I can most al'ays tell about Jocelyn's as good as the Weather Report. I told Mrs. Maynard here this mornin' that the fog was goin' to burn off."

"Burn off?" cried Mrs. Alger. "I should think it had!" The other ladies laughed.

"And you'll see," added Barlow, "that the wind'll change at noon, and we'll have it cooler."

"If it's as hot on the water as it is here," said Mrs. Scott, "I should think those people would get a sunstroke."

"Well, so should I, Mrs. Scott," cordially exclaimed a little fat lady, as if here at last were an opinion in which all might rejoice to sympathize.

"It's never so hot on the water, Mrs. Merritt," said Mrs. Alger, with the instructiveness of an old habitue.

"Well, not at Jocelyn's," suggested Barlow. Mrs. Alger stopped fanning herself with her newspaper, and looked at him. Upon her motion, the other ladies looked at Barlow. Doubtless he felt that his social acceptability had ceased with his immediate usefulness. But he appeared resolved to carry it off easily. "Well," he said, "I suppose I must go and pick my peas."

No one said anything to this. When the factotum had disappeared round the corner of the house, Mrs. Alger turned her head' aside, and glanced downward with an air of fatigue. In this manner Barlow was dismissed from the ladies' minds.

"I presume," said young Mrs. Scott, with a deferential glance at Grace, "that the sun is good for a person with lung-difficulty."

Grace silently refused to consider herself appealed to, and Mrs. Merritt said, "Better than the moon, I should think."

Some of the others tittered, but Grace looked up at Mrs. Merritt and said, "I don't think Mrs. Maynard's case is so bad that she need be afraid of either."

"Oh, I am so glad to hear it!" replied the other. She looked round, but was unable to form a party. By twos or threes they might have liked to take Mrs. Maynard to pieces; but no one cares to make unkind remarks before a whole company of people. Some of the ladies even began to say pleasant things about Mr. Libby, as if he were Grace's friend.

"I always like to see these fair men when they get tanned," said Mrs. Alger. "Their blue eyes look so very blue. And the backs of their necks - just like my boys!"

"Do you admire such a VERY fighting-clip as Mr. Libby has on?" asked Mrs. Scott.

"It must be nice for summer," returned the elder lady.

"Yes, it certainly must," admitted the younger.

"Really," said another, "I wish I could go in the fighting-clip. One doesn't know what to do with one's hair at the sea-side; it's always in the way."

"Your hair would be a public loss, Mrs. Frost," said Mrs. Alger. The others looked at her hair, as if they had seen it now for the first time.

"Oh, I don't think so," said Mrs. Frost, in a sort of flattered coo.

"Oh, don't have it cut off!" pleaded a young girl, coming up and taking the beautiful mane, hanging loose after the bath, into her hand. Mrs. Frost put her arm round the girl's waist, and pulled her down against her shoulder. Upon reflection she also kissed her.

Through a superstition, handed down from mother to daughter, that it is uncivil and even unkind not to keep saying something, they went on talking vapidities, where the same number of men, equally vacuous, would have remained silent; and some of them complained that the nervous strain of conversation took away all the good their bath had done them. Miss Gleason, who did not bathe, was also not a talker. She kept a bright-eyed reticence, but was apt to break out in rather enigmatical flashes, which resolved the matter in hand into an abstraction, and left the others with the feeling that she was a person of advanced ideas, but that, while rejecting historical Christianity, she believed in a God of Love. This Deity was said, upon closer analysis, to have proved to be a God of

Sentiment, and Miss Gleason was herself a hero-worshiper, or, more strictly speaking, a heroine-worshiper. At present Dr. Breen was her cult, and she was apt to lie in wait for her idol, to beam upon it with her suggestive eyes, and evidently to expect it to say or do something remarkable, but not to suffer anything like disillusion or disappointment in any event. She would sometimes offer it suddenly a muddled depth of sympathy in such phrases as, "Too bad!" or, "I don't see how you keep-up?" and darkly insinuate that she appreciated all that Grace was doing. She seemed to rejoice in keeping herself at a respectful distance, to which she breathlessly retired, as she did now, after waylaying her at the top of the stairs, and confidentially darting at her the words, "I'm so glad you don't like scandal!"

William Dean Howells

III

After dinner the ladies tried to get a nap, but such of them as re-appeared on the piazza later agreed that it was perfectly useless. They tested every corner for a breeze, but the wind had fallen dead, and the vast sweep of sea seemed to smoulder under the sun. "This is what Mr. Barlow calls having it cooler," said Mrs. Alger.

"There are some clouds that look like thunderheads in the west," said Mrs. Frost, returning from an excursion to the part of the piazza commanding that quarter.

"Oh, it won't rain to-day," Mrs. Alger decided.

"I thought there was always a breeze at Jocelyn's," Mrs. Scott observed, in the critical spirit of a recent arrival.

"There always is," the other explained, "except the first week you're here."

A little breath, scarcely more than a sentiment of breeze, made itself felt. "I do believe the wind has changed," said Mrs. Frost. "It's east." The others owned one by one that it was so, and she enjoyed the merit of a discoverer; but her discovery was rapidly superseded. The clouds mounted in the west, and there came a time when the ladies disputed whether they had heard thunder or not: a faction contended for the bowling alley, and another faction held for a wagon passing over the bridge just before you reached Jocelyn's. But those who were faithful to the theory of thunder carried the day by a sudden crash that broke over the forest, and, dying slowly away among the low hills, left them deeply silent.

"Some one," said Mrs. Alger, "ought to go for those children." On this it appeared that there were two minds as to where the children were, - whether on the beach or in the woods.

"Wasn't that thunder, Grace?" asked Mrs. Breen, with the accent by which she implicated her daughter in whatever happened.

"Yes," said Grace, from where she sat at her window, looking seaward, and waiting tremulously for her mother's next question.

"Where is Mrs. Maynard?"

"She isn't back, yet."

"Then," said Mrs. Breen, "he really did expect rough weather."

"He must," returned Grace, in a guilty whisper.

"It's a pity," remarked her mother, "that you made them go."

"Yes." She rose, and, stretching herself far out of the window, searched the inexorable expanse of sea. It had already darkened at the verge, and the sails of some fishing-craft flecked a livid wall with their white, but there was no small boat in sight.

"If anything happened to them," her mother continued, "I should feel terribly for you."

"I should feel terribly for myself," Grace responded, with her eyes still seaward.

"Where do you think they went?"

"I didn't ask," said the girl. "I wouldn't," she added, in devotion to the whole truth.

"Well, it is all of the same piece," said Mrs. Breen. Grace did not ask what the piece was. She remained staring at the dark wall across the sea, and spiritually confronting her own responsibility, no atom of which she rejected. She held herself in every way responsible, - for doubting that poor young fellow's word, and then for forcing that reluctant creature to go with him, and forbidding by her fierce insistence any attempt of his at explanation; she condemned herself to perpetual remorse with even greater zeal than her mother would have sentenced her, and she would not permit herself any respite when a little sail, which she knew for theirs, blew round the point. It seemed to fly along just on the hither side of that mural darkness, skilfully tacking to reach the end of the-reef before the wall pushed it on the rocks. Suddenly, the long low stretch of the reef broke into white foam, and then passed from sight under the black wall, against which the little sail still flickered. The girl fetched a long, silent breath. They were inside the reef, in comparatively smooth water, and to her ignorance they were safe. But the rain would be coming in another moment, and Mrs. Maynard would be drenched; and Grace would be to blame for her death. She ran to the closet, and pulled down her mother's India-rubber cloak and her own, and fled out-of-doors, to be ready on the beach with the wrap, against their landing. She met the other ladies on the stairs and in the hall, and they clamored at her; but she glided through them like something in a dream, and then she heard a shouting in her ear, and felt herself caught and held up against the wind.

"Where in land be you goin', Miss Breen?"

Barlow, in a long, yellow oil-skin coat and sou'wester hat, kept pushing her forward to the edge of the cliff, as he asked.

"I'm going down to meet them!" she screamed.

"Well, I hope you WILL meet 'em. But I guess you better go back to the house. Hey? WUNT? Well; come along, then, if they ain't past doctorin' by the time they git ashore! Pretty well wrapped up, any way!" he roared; and she perceived that she had put on her waterproof and drawn the hood over her head.

Those steps to the beach had made her giddy when she descended with leisure for such dismay; but now, with the tempest flattening her against the stair-case, and her gossamer clutching and clinging to every surface, and again twisting itself about her limbs, she clambered down as swiftly and recklessly as Barlow himself, and followed over the beach beside the men who were pulling a boat down the sand at a run.

"Let me get in!" she screamed. "I wish to go with you!"

"Take hold of the girl, Barlow!" shouted one of the men. "She's crazy."

He tumbled himself with four others into the boat, and they all struck out together through the froth and swirl of the waves. She tried to free herself from Barlow, so as to fling the waterproof into the boat. "Take this, then. She'll be soaked through!"

Barlow broke into a grim laugh. "She won't need it, except for a windin'-sheet!" he roared. "Don't you see the boat's drivin' right on t' the sand? She'll be kindlin' wood in a minute."

"But they're inside the reef! They can come to anchor!" she shrieked in reply. He answered her with a despairing grin and a shake of the head. "They can't. What has your boat gone out for, then?"

"To pick 'em up out the sea. But they'll never git 'em alive. Look how she slaps her boom int' the water! Well! He DOES know how to handle a boat!"

It was Libby at the helm, as she could dimly see, but what it was in his management that moved Barlow's praise she could not divine. The boat seemed to be aimed for the shore, and to be rushing, head on, upon the beach; her broad sail was blown straight out over her bow, and flapped there like a banner, while the heavy boom hammered the water as she rose and fell. A jagged line of red seamed the breast of the dark wall behind; a rending crash came, and as if fired upon, the boat flung up her sail, as a wild fowl flings up its wing when shot, and lay tossing keel up, on the top of the waves. It all looked scarcely a stone's cast away, though it was vastly farther. A figure was seen to drag itself up out of the sea, and fall over into the boat, hovering and pitching in the surrounding welter, and struggling to get at two other figures clinging to the wreck. Suddenly the men in the boat pulled away, and Grace uttered a cry of despair and reproach: "Why, they're leaving it, they're leaving it!"

"Don't expect 'em to tow the wreck ashore in this weather, do ye?" shouted Barlow. "They've got the folks all safe enough. I tell ye I see 'em!" he cried, at a wild look of doubt in her eyes. "Run to the house, there, and get everything in apple-pie order. There's goin' to be a chance for some of your doctor'n' now, if ye know how to fetch folks to."

It was the little house on the beach, which the children were always prying and peering into, trying the lock, and wondering what the boat was like, which Grace had seen launched. Now the door yielded to her, and within she found a fire kindled in the stove, blankets laid in order, and flasks of brandy in readiness in the cupboard. She put the blankets to heat for instant use, and prepared for the work of resuscitation. When she could turn from them to the door, she met there a procession that approached with difficulty, heads down and hustled by the furious blast through which the rain now hissed and shot. Barlow and one of the boat's crew were carrying Mrs. Maynard, and bringing up the rear of the huddling oil-skins and sou'westers came Libby, soaked, and dripping as he walked. His eyes and Grace's encountered with a mutual avoidance; but whatever was their sense of blame, their victim had no reproaches to make herself. She was not in need of restoration. She was perfectly alive, and apparently stimulated by her escape from deadly peril to a vivid conception of the wrong that had been done her. If the adventure had passed off prosperously, she was the sort of woman to have owned to her friend that she ought not to have thought of going. But the event had obliterated these scruples, and she realized herself as a hapless creature who had been thrust on to dangers from which she would have shrunk. "Well, Grace!" she began, with a voice and look before which the other quailed, "I hope you are satisfied! All the time I was clinging to that wretched boat. I was wondering how you would feel. Yes, my last thoughts were of you. I pitied you. I didn't see how you could ever have peace again."

"Hold on, Mrs. Maynard!" cried Libby. "There's no, time for that, now. What had best be done, Miss Green? Hadn't she better be got up to the house?"

"Yes, by all means," answered Grace.

"You might as well let me die here," Mrs. Maynard protested, as Grace wrapped the blankets round her dripping dress. "I 'm as wet as I can be, now."

Libby began to laugh at these inconsequences, to which he was probably well used. "You wouldn't have time to die here. And we want to give this hydropathic treatment a fair trial. You've tried the douche, and now you're to have the pack." He summoned two of the boatmen, who had been considerately dripping outside, in order to leave the interior to the shipwrecked company, and they lifted Mrs. Maynard, finally wrapped in, Grace's India-rubber cloak, and looking like some sort of strange, huge chrysalis, and carried her out into the storm and up the steps.

Grace followed last with Mr. Libby, very heavyhearted and reckless. She had not only that sore self-accusal; but the degradation of the affair, its grotesqueness, its spiritual squalor, its utter gracelessness, its entire want of dignity, were bitter as death in her proud soul. It was not in this shameful guise that she had foreseen the good she was to do. And it had all come through her own wilfulness and self-righteousness. The tears could mix unseen with the rain that drenched her face, but they blinded her, and half-way up the steps she stumbled on her skirt, and would have fallen, if the young man had not caught her. After that, from time to time he put his arm about her, and stayed her against the gusts.

Before they reached the top he said, "Miss Breen, I'm awfully sorry for all this. Mrs. Maynard will be ashamed of what she said. Confound it! If Maynard were only here!"

"Why should she be ashamed?" demanded Grace. "If she had been drowned, I should have murdered her, and I'm responsible if anything happens to her, - I am to blame." She escaped from him, and ran into the house. He slunk round the piazza to the kitchen door, under the eyes of the ladies watching at the parlor windows.

"I wonder he let the others carry her up," said Miss Gleason. "Of course, he will marry her now, - when she gets her divorce." She spoke of Mrs. Maynard, whom her universal toleration not only included in the mercy which the opinions of the other ladies denied her, but round whom her romance cast a halo of pretty possibilities as innocently sentimental as the hopes of a young girl.

IV

The next morning Grace was sitting beside her patient, with whom she had spent the night. It was possibly Mrs. Maynard's spiritual toughness which availed her, for she did not seem much the worse for her adventure: she had a little fever, and she was slightly hoarser; but she had died none of the deaths that she projected during the watches of the night, and for which she had chastened the spirit of her physician by the repeated assurance that she forgave her everything, and George Maynard everything, and hoped that they would be good to her poor little Bella. She had the child brought from its crib to her own bed, and moaned over it; but with the return of day and the duties of life she appeared to feel that she had carried her forgiveness far enough, and was again remembering her injuries against Grace, as she lay in her morning gown on the lounge which had been brought in for her from the parlor.

"Yes, Grace, I shall always say if I had died and I may die yet - that I did not wish to go out with Mr. Libby, and that I went purely to please you. You forced me to go. I can't understand why you did it; for I don't suppose you wanted to kill us, whatever you did."

Grace could not lift her head. She bowed it over the little girl whom she had on her knee, and who was playing with the pin at her throat, in apparent unconsciousness of all that was said. But she had really followed it, with glimpses of intelligence, as children do, and now at this negative accusal she lifted her hand, and suddenly struck Grace a stinging blow on the cheek.

William Dean Howells

Mrs. Maynard sprang from her lounge. "Why, Bella! you worthless little wretch!" She caught her from Grace's knee, and shook her violently. Then, casting the culprit from her at random, she flung herself down again in a fit of coughing, while the child fled to Grace for consolation, and, wildly sobbing, buried her face in the lap of her injured friend.

"I don't know what I shall do about that child!" cried Mrs. Maynard. "She has George Maynard's temper right over again. I feel dreadfully, Grace!"

"Oh, never mind it," said Grace, fondling the child, and half addressing it. "I suppose Bella thought I had been unkind to her mother."

"That's just it!" exclaimed Louise. "When you've been kindness itself! Don't I owe everything to you? I shouldn't be alive at this moment if it were not for your treatment. Oh, Grace!" She began to cough again; the paroxysm increased in vehemence. She caught her handkerchief from her lips; it was spotted with blood. She sprang to her feet, and regarded it with impersonal sternness. "Now," she said, "I am sick, and I want a doctor!"

"A doctor," Grace meekly echoed.

"Yes. I can't be trifled with any longer. I want a man doctor!"

Grace had looked at the handkerchief. "Very well," she said, with coldness. "I shall not stand in your way of calling another physician. But if it will console you, I can tell you that the blood on your handkerchief means nothing worth speaking of. Whom shall I send for?" she asked, turning to go out of the roam. "I wish to be your friend still, and I will do anything I can to help you."

"Oh, Grace Breen! Is that the way you talk to me?" whimpered Mrs. Maynard. "You know that I don't mean to give you up. I'm not a stone; I have some feeling. I didn't intend to dismiss you, but I thought perhaps you would like to have a consultation about it. I should think it was time to have a consultation, shouldn't you? Of course, I'm not alarmed, but I know it's getting serious, and I'm afraid that your medicine isn't active enough. That's it; it's perfectly good medicine, but it isn't active. They've all been saying that I ought to have something active. Why not try the whiskey with the white-pine chips in it? I'm sure it's indicated." In her long course of medication she had picked up certain professional phrases, which she used with amusing seriousness. "It would be active, at any rate."

Grace did not reply. As she stood smoothing the head of the little girl, who had followed her to the door, and now leaned against her, hiding her tearful face in Grace's dress, she said, "I don't know of any homoeopathic physician in this neighborhood. I don't believe there's one nearer than Boston, and I should make myself ridiculous in calling one so far for a consultation. But I'm quite willing you should call one, and I will send for you at once."

"And wouldn't you consult with him, after he came?"

"Certainly not. It would be absurd."

"I shouldn't like to have a doctor come all the way from Boston," mused Mrs. Maynard, sinking on the lounge again. "There must be a doctor in the neighborhood. It can't be so healthy as that!"

"There's an allopathic physician at Corbitant," said Grace passively. "A very good one, I believe," she added.

"Oh, well, then!" cried Mrs. Maynard, with immense relief. "Consult with him!"

"I've told you, Louise, that I would not consult with anybody. And I certainly wouldn't consult with a physician whose ideas and principles I knew nothing about."

William Dean Howells

"Why but, Grace," Mrs. Maynard expostulated. "Isn't that rather prejudiced?" She began to take an impartial interest in Grace's position, and fell into an argumentative tone. "If two heads are better than one, - and everybody says they are, - I don't see how you can consistently refuse to talk with another physician."

"I can't explain to you, Louise," said Grace. "But you can call Dr. Mulbridge, if you wish. That will be the right way for you to do, if you have lost confidence in me."

"I haven't lost confidence in you, Grace. I don't see how you can talk so. You can give me bread pills, if you like, or air pills, and I will take them gladly. I believe in you perfectly. But I do think that in a matter of this kind, where my health, and perhaps my life, is concerned, I ought to have a little say. I don't ask you to give up your principles, and I don't dream of giving you up, and yet you won't just to please me! - exchange a few words with another doctor about my case, merely because he's allopathic. I should call it bigotry, and I don't see how you can call it anything else." There was a sound of voices at the door outside, and she called cheerily, "Come in, Mr. Libby, - come in! There's nobody but Grace here," she added, as the young man tentatively opened the door, and looked in. He wore an evening dress, even to the white cravat, and he carried in his hand a crush hat: there was something anomalous in his appearance, beyond the phenomenal character of his costume, and he blushed consciously as he bowed to Grace, and then at her motion shook hands with her. Mrs. Maynard did not give herself the fatigue of rising; she stretched her hand to him from the lounge, and he took it without the joy which he had shown when Grace made him the same advance. "How very swell you look. Going to an evening party this morning?" she cried; and after she had given him a second glance of greater intensity, "Why, what in the world has come over' you?" It was the dress which Mr. Libby wore. He was a young fellow far too well made, and carried himself too alertly, to look as if any clothes misfitted him; his person gave their good cut elegance, but he had the effect of having fallen away in them. "Why, you look as if you had been sick a month!" Mrs. Maynard interpreted.

The young man surveyed himself with a downward glance. "They're Johnson's," he explained. "He had them down for a hop at the Long Beach House, and sent over for them. I had nothing but my camping flannels, and they haven't been got into shape yet, since yesterday. I wanted to come over and see how you were."

"Poor fellow!" exclaimed Mrs. Maynard. "I never thought of you! How in the world did you get to your camp?"

"I walked."

"In all that rain?"

"Well, I had been pretty well sprinkled, already. It wasn't a question of wet and dry; it was a question of wet and wet. I was going off bareheaded, I lost my hat in the water, you know, - but your man, here, hailed me round the corner of the kitchen, and lent me one. I've been taking up collections of clothes ever since."

Mr. Libby spoke lightly, and with a cry of "Barlow's hat!" Mrs. Maynard went off in a shriek of laughter; but a deep distress kept Grace silent. It seemed to her that she had been lacking not only in thoughtfulness, but in common humanity, in suffering him to walk away several miles in the rain, without making an offer to keep him and have him provided for in the house. She remembered now her bewildered impression that he was without a hat when he climbed the stairs and helped her to the house; she recalled the fact that she had thrust him on to the danger he had escaped, and her heart was melted with grief and shame. "Mr. Libby" - she began, going up to him, and drooping before him in an attitude which simply and frankly expressed the contrition she felt; but she could not continue. Mrs. Maynard's laugh broke into the usual cough, and as soon as she could speak she seized the word.

William Dean Howells

"Well, there, now; we can leave it to Mr. Libby. It's the principle of the thing that I look at. And I want to see how it strikes him. I want to know, Mr. Libby, if you were a doctor," - he looked at Grace, and flushed, - "and a person was very sick, and wanted you to consult with another doctor, whether you would let the mere fact that you hadn't been introduced have any weight with you?" The young man silently appealed to Grace, who darkened angrily, and before he could speak Mrs. Maynard interposed. "No, no, you sha'n't ask her. I want your opinion. It's just an abstract question." She accounted for this fib with a wink at Grace.

"Really," he said, "it's rather formidable. I've never been a doctor of any kind."

"Oh, yes, we know that!" said Mrs. Maynard. "But you are now, and now would you do it?"

"If the other fellow knew more, I would."

"But if you thought he didn't?"

"Then I wouldn't. What are you trying to get at, Mrs. Maynard? I'm not going to answer any more of your questions."

"Yes, - one more. Don't you think it's a doctor's place to get his patient well any way he can?"

"Why, of course!"

"There, Grace! It's just exactly the same case. And ninety-nine out of a hundred would decide against you every time."

Libby turned towards Grace in confusion. "Miss Breen - I didn't understand - I don't presume to meddle in anything - You're not fair, Mrs. Maynard! I haven't any opinion on the subject, Miss Breen; I haven't, indeed!"

"Oh, you can't back out, now!" exclaimed Mrs. Maynard joyously. "You've said it."

"And you're quite right, Mr. Libby," said Grace haughtily. She bade him good-morning; but he followed her from the room, and left Mrs. Maynard to her triumph.

"Miss Breen - Do let me speak to you, please! Upon my word and honor, I didn't know what she was driving at; I didn't, indeed! It's pretty rough on me, for I never dreamt of setting myself up as a judge of your affairs. I know you're right, whatever you think; and I take it all back; it was got out of me by fraud, any way. And I beg your pardon for not calling you Doctor - if you want me to do it. The other comes more natural; but I wish to recognize you in the way you prefer, for I do feel most respectul - reverent - "

He was so very earnest and so really troubled, and he stumbled about so for the right word, and hit upon the wrong one with such unfailing disaster, that she must have been superhuman not to laugh. Her laughing seemed to relieve him even more than her hearty speech. "Call me how you like, Mr. Libby. I don't insist upon anything with you; but I believe I prefer Miss Breen."

"You're very kind! Miss Breen it is, then. And you'll forgive my siding against you?" he demanded radiantly.

"Don't speak of that again, please. I've nothing to forgive you."

They walked down-stairs and out on the piazza. Barlow stood before the steps, holding by the bit a fine bay mare, who twitched her head round a little at the sound of Libby's voice, and gave him a look. He passed without noticing the horse. "I'm glad to find Mrs. Maynard so well. With that cold of hers, hanging on so long, I didn't know but she'd be in an awful state this morning."

"Yes," said Grace, "it's a miraculous escape."

"The fact is I sent over to New Leyden for my team yesterday. I didn't know how things might turn out, and you're so far from a lemon here, that I thought I might be useful in going errands."

Grace turned her head and glanced at the equipage. "Is that your team?"

"Yes," said the young fellow, with a smile of suppressed pride.

"What an exquisite creature!" said the girl.

"ISN'T she?" They both faced about, and stood looking at the mare, and the light, shining, open buggy behind her. The sunshine had the after-storm glister; the air was brisk, and the breeze blew balm from the heart of the pine forest. "Miss Breen," he broke out, "I wish you'd take a little dash through the woods with me. I've got a broad-track buggy, that's just right for these roads. I don't suppose it's the thing at all to ask you, on such short acquaintance, but I wish you would. I know you'd enjoy it: Come?"

His joyous urgence gave her a strange thrill. She had long ceased to imagine herself the possible subject of what young ladies call attentions, and she did not think of herself in that way now. There was something in the frank, eager boyishness of the invitation that fascinated her, and the sunny face turned so hopefully upon her had its amusing eloquence. She looked about the place with an anxiety of which she was immediately ashamed: all the ladies were out of sight, and probably at the foot of the cliff.

"Don't say no, Miss Breen," pleaded the gay voice.

The answer seemed to come of itself. "Oh, thank you, yes, I should like to go."

"Good!" he exclaimed, and the word which riveted her consent made her recoil.

"But not this morning. Some other day. I - I - I want to think about Mrs. Maynard. I - oughtn't to leave her. Excuse me this morning, Mr. Libby."

"Why, of course," he tried to say with unaltered gayety, but a note of disappointment made itself felt. "Do you think she's going to be worse?"

"No, I don't think she is. But - " She paused, and waited a space before she continued. "I'm afraid I can't be of use to her any longer. She has lost confidence in me - It's important she should trust her physician." Libby blushed, as he always did when required to recognize Grace in her professional quality. "It's more a matter of nerves than anything else, and if she doesn't believe in me I can't do her any good."

"Yes, I can understand that," said the young man, with gentle sympathy; and she felt, somehow, that he delicately refrained from any leading or prompting comment.

"She has been urging me to have a consultation with some doctor about her case, and I - it would be ridiculous!"

"Then I wouldn't do it!" said Mr. Libby. "You know a great deal better what she wants than she does. You had better make her, do what you say."

"I didn't mean to burden you with my affairs," said Grace, "but I wished to explain her motive in speaking to you as she did." After she had said this, it seemed to her rather weak, and she could not think of anything else that would strengthen it. The young man might think that she had asked advice of him. She began to resent his telling her to make Mrs. Maynard do what she said. She was about to add something to snub him, when she recollected that it was her own wilfulness which had precipitated the present situation, and she humbled herself.

"She will probably change her mind," said Libby. "She would if you could let her carry her point," he added, with a light esteem for Mrs. Maynard which set him wrong again in Grace's eyes: he had no business to speak so to her.

"Very likely," she said, in stiff withdrawal from all terms of confidence concerning Mrs. Maynard. She did not add anything more, and she meant that the young fellow should perceive that his, audience was at an end. He did not apparently resent it, but she fancied him hurt in his acquiescence.

She went back to her patient, whom she found languid and disposed to sleep after the recent excitement, and she left her again, taking little Bella with her. Mrs. Maynard slept long, but woke none the better for her nap. Towards evening she grew feverish, and her fever mounted as the night fell. She was restless and wakeful, and between her dreamy dozes she was incessant in her hints for a consultation to Grace, who passed the night in her room, and watched every change for the worse with a self-accusing heart. The impending trouble was in that indeterminate phase which must give the physician his most anxious moments; and this inexperienced girl; whose knowledge was all to be applied, and who had hardly arrived yet at that dismaying stage when a young physician finds all the results at war with all the precepts, began to realize the awfulness of her responsibility. She had always thought of saving life, and not of losing it.

V

By morning Grace was as nervous and anxious as her patient, who had momentarily the advantage of her in having fallen asleep. She went stealthily out, and walked the length of the piazza, bathing her eyes with the sight of the sea, cool and dim under a clouded sky. At the corner next the kitchen she encountered Barlow, who, having kindled the fire for the cook, had spent s moment of leisure in killing some chickens at the barn; he appeared with a cluster of his victims in his hand, but at sight of Grace he considerately put them behind him.

She had not noticed them. "Mr. Barlow," she said, "how far is it to Corbitant?"

Barlow slouched into a conversational posture, easily resting on his raised hip the back of the hand in which he held the chickens. "Well, it's accordin' to who you ask. Some says six mile, and real clever folks makes it about four and a quarter."

"I ask you," persisted Grace.

"Well, the last time I was there, I thought it was about sixty. 'Most froze my fingers goin' round the point. 'N' all I was afraid of was gettin' there too soon. Tell you, a lee shore ain't a pleasant neighbor in a regular old northeaster. 'F you go by land, I guess it's about ten mile round through the woods. Want to send for Dr. Mulbridge? I thought mebbe" -

"No, no!" said Grace. She turned back into the house, and

William Dean Howells

then she came running out again; but by this time Barlow had gone into the kitchen, where she heard him telling the cook that these were the last of the dommyneckers. At breakfast several of the ladies came and asked after Mrs. Maynard, whose restless night they had somehow heard of. When she came out of the dining-room' Miss Gleason waylaid her in the hall.

"Dr. Breen," she said, in a repressed tumult, "I hope you won't give way. For woman's sake, I hope you won't! You owe it to yourself not to give way! I'm sure Mrs. Maynard is as well off in your hands she can be. If I didn't think so, I should be the last to advise your being firm; but, feeling as I do, I do advise it most strongly. Everything depends on it."

"I don't know what you mean, Miss Gleason," said Grace.

"I'm glad it hasn't come to you yet. If it was a question of mere professional pride, I should say, By all means call him at once. But I feel that a great deal more is involved. If you yield, you make it harder for other women to help themselves hereafter, and you confirm such people as these in their distrust of female physicians. Looking at it in a large way, I almost feel that it would be better for her to die than for you to give up; and feeling as I do" -

"Are you talking of Mrs. Maynard?" asked Grace.

"They are all saying that you ought to give up the case to Dr. Mulbridge. But I hope you won't. I shouldn't blame you for calling in another female physician" -

"Thank you," answered Grace. "There is no danger of her dying. But it seems to me that she has too many female physicians already. In this house I should think it better to call a man." She left the barb to rankle in Miss Gleason's breast, and followed her mother to her room, who avenged Miss Gleason by a series of inquisitional tortures, ending with the hope that, whatever she did, Grace would not have that silly creature's blood on her hands. The girl opened her lips to attempt some answer to this unanswerable aspiration, when the unwonted sound of wheels on the road without caught her ear.

"What is that, Grace?" demanded her mother, as if Grace were guilty of the noise.

"Mr. Libby," answered Grace, rising.

"Has he come for you?"

"I don't know. But I am going down to see him."

At sight of the young man's face, Grace felt her heart lighten. He had jumped from his buggy, and was standing at his smiling ease on the piazza steps, looking about as if for some one, and he brightened joyfully at her coming. He took her hand with eager friendliness, and at her impulse began to move away to the end of the piazza with her. The ladies had not yet descended to the beach; apparently their interest in Dr. Breen's patient kept them.

"How is Mrs. Maynard this morning?" he asked; and she answered, as they got beyond earshot, -

"Not better, I'm afraid."

"Oh, I'm sorry," said the young man. "Then you won't be able to drive with me this morning? I hope she isn't seriously worse?" he added, recurring to Mrs. Maynard at the sight of the trouble in Grace's face.

"I shall ask to drive with you," she returned. "Mr. Libby, do you know where Corbitant is?"

"Oh, yes."

"And will you drive me there?"

"Why, certainly!" he cried, in polite wonder.

"Thank you." She turned half round, and cast a woman's look at the other women. "I shall be ready in half an hour. Will you go away, and comeback then? Not sooner."

"Anything you please, Miss Breen," he said, laughing in his mystification. "In thirty minutes, or thirty days."

They went back to the steps, and he mounted his buggy. She sat down, and taking some work from her pocket, bent her head over it. At first she was pale, and then she grew red. But these fluctuations of color could not keep her spectators long; one by one they dispersed and descended the cliff; and when she rose to go for her hat the last had vanished, with a longing look at her. It was Miss Gleason.

Grace briefly announced her purpose to her mother, who said, "I hope you are not doing anything impulsive"; and she answered, "No, I had quite made up my mind to it last night."

Mr. Libby had not yet returned when she went back to the piazza, and she walked out on the road by which he must arrive. She had not to walk far. He drew in sight before she had gone a quarter of a mile, driving rapidly. "Am I late?" he asked, turning, and pulling up at the roadside, with well-subdued astonishment at encountering her.

"Oh, no; not that I know." She mounted to the seat, and they drove off in a silence which endured for a long time. If Libby had been as vain as he seemed light, he must have found it cruelly unflattering, for it ignored his presence and even his existence. She broke the silence at last with a deep-drawn sigh, as frankly sad as if she had been quite alone, but she returned to consciousness of him in it. "Mr. Libby, you must think it is very strange for me to ask you to drive me to Corbitant without troubling myself to tell you my errand."

"Oh, not at all," said the young man. "I'm glad to be of use on any terms. It isn't often that one gets the chance."

"I am going to see Dr. Mulbridge," she began, and then stopped so long that he perceived she wished him to say something.

He said, "Yes?"

"Yes. I thought this morning that I should give Mrs. Maynard's case up to him. I shouldn't be at all troubled at seeming to give it up under a pressure of opinion, though I should not give it up for that. Of course," she explained, "you don't know that all those women have been saying that I ought to call in Dr. Mulbridge. It's one of those things," she added bitterly, "that make it so pleasant for a woman to try to help women." He made a little murmur of condolence, and she realized that she had thrown herself on his sympathy, when she thought she had been merely thinking aloud. "What I mean is that he is a man of experience and reputation, and could probably be of more use to her than I, for she would trust him more. But I have known her a long time, and I understand her temperament and her character, - which goes for a good deal in such matters, - and I have concluded not to give up the case. I wish to meet Dr. Mulbridge, however, and ask him to see her in consultation with me. That is all," she ended rather haughtily, as if she had been dramatizing the fact to Dr. Mulbridge in her own mind.

"I should think that would be the right thing," said Libby limply, with uncalled-for approval; but he left this dangerous ground abruptly. "As you say, character goes for a great deal in these things. I've seen Mrs. Maynard at the point of death before. As a general rule, she doesn't die. If you have known her a long time, you know what I mean. She likes to share her sufferings with her friends. I've seen poor old Maynard" -

"Mr. Libby!" Grace broke in. "You may speak of Mr. Maynard as you like, but I cannot allow your disrespectfulness to Mrs. Maynard. It's shocking! You had no right to be their friend if

William Dean Howells

you felt toward them as you seem to have done."

"Why, there was no harm in them. I liked them!" explained the young man.

"People have no right to like those they don't respect!"

Libby looked as if this were rather a new and droll idea. But he seemed not to object to her tutoring him. "Well," he said, "as far as Mrs. Maynard was concerned, I don't know that I liked her any more than I respected her."

Grace ought to have frowned at this, but she had to check a smile in. order to say gravely, "I know she is disagreeable at times. And she likes to share her sufferings with others, as you say. But her husband was fully entitled to any share of them that he may have borne. If he had been kinder to her, she wouldn't be what and where she is now."

"Kinder to her!" Libby exclaimed. "He's the kindest fellow in the world! Now, Miss Breen," he said earnestly, "I hope Mrs. Maynard hasn't been talking against her husband to you?"

"Is it possible," demanded Grace, "that you don't know they're separated, and that she's going to take steps for a divorce?"

"A divorce? No! What in the world for?"

"I never talk gossip. I thought of course she had told you" -

"She never told me a word! She was ashamed to do it! She knows that I know Maynard was the best husband in the world to her. All she told me was that he was out on his ranch, and she had come on here for her health. It's some ridiculous little thing that no reasonable woman would have dreamt of caring for. It's one of her caprices. It's her own fickleness. She's tired of him, - or thinks she is, and that's all about it. Miss Breen, I beg you won't believe anything against Maynard!"

"I don't understand," faltered Grace, astonished at his fervor; and the light it cast upon her first doubts of him. "Of course, I only know the affair from her report, and I haven't concerned myself in it, except as it affected her health. And I don't wish to misjudge him. And I like your - defending him," she said, though it instantly seemed a patronizing thing to have said. "But I couldn't withhold my sympathy where I believed there had been neglect and systematic unkindness, and finally desertion."

"Oh, I know Mrs. Maynard; I know her kind of talk. I've seen Maynard's neglect and unkindness, and I know just what his desertion would be. If he's left her, it's because she wanted him to leave her; he did it to humor her, to please her. I shall have a talk with Mrs. Maynard when we get back."

"I 'm afraid I can't allow it at present," said Grace, very seriously.

"She is worse to-day. Otherwise I shouldn't be giving you this trouble."

"Oh, it's no trouble" - "But I'm glad - I'm glad we've had this understanding. I'm very glad. It makes me think worse of myself and better of - others."

Libby gave a laugh. "And you like that? You're easily pleased."

She remained grave. "I ought to be able to tell you what I mean. But it isn't possible - now. Will you let me beg your pardon?" she urged, with impulsive earnestness.

"Why, yes," he answered, smiling.

"And not ask me why?"

"Certainly."

"Thank you. Yes," she added hastily, "she is so much worse

that some one of greater experience than I must see her, and I have made up my mind. Dr. Mulbridge may refuse to consult with me. I know very well that there is a prejudice against women physicians, and I couldn't especially blame him for sharing it. I have thought it all over. If he refuses, I shall know what to do." She had ceased to address Libby, who respected her soliloquy. He drove on rapidly over the soft road, where the wheels made no sound, and the track wandered with apparent aimlessness through the interminable woods of young oak and pine. The low trees were full of the sunshine, and dappled them with shadow as they dashed along; the fresh, green ferns springing from the brown carpet of the pine-needles were as if painted against it. The breath of the pines was heavier for the recent rain; and the woody smell of the oaks was pungent where the balsam failed. They met no one, but the solitude did not make itself felt through her preoccupation. From time to time she dropped a word or two; but for the most she was silent, and he did not attempt to lead. By and by they came to an opener place, where there were many red field-lilies tilting in the wind.

"Would you like some of those?" he asked, pulling up.

"I should, very much," she answered, glad of the sight of the gay things. But when he had gathered her a bunch of the flowers she looked down at them in her lap, and said, "It's silly in me to be caring for lilies at such a time, and I should make an unfavorable impression on Dr. Mulbridge if he saw me with them. But I shall risk their effect on him. He may think I have been botanizing."

"Unless you tell him you haven't," the young man suggested.

"I needn't do that."

"I don't think any one else would do it."

She colored a little at the tribute to her candor, and it pleased her, though it had just pleased her as much to forget that she was not like any other young girl who might be simply and irresponsibly happy in flowers gathered for her by a young man. "I won't tell him, either!" she cried, willing to grasp the fleeting emotion again; but it was gone, and only a little residue of sad consciousness remained.

The woods gave way on either side of the road, which began to be a village street, sloping and shelving down toward the curve of a quiet bay. The neat weather-gray dwellings, shingled to the ground and brightened with door-yard flowers and creepers, straggled off into the boat-houses and fishing-huts on the shore, and the village seemed to get afloat at last in the sloops and schooners riding in the harbor, whose smooth plane rose higher to the eye than the town itself. The salt and the sand were everywhere, but though there had been no positive prosperity in Corbitant for a generation, the place had an impregnable neatness, which defied decay; if there had been a dog in the street, there would not have been a stick to throw at him.

One of the better, but not the best, of the village houses, which did not differ from the others in any essential particular, and which stood flush upon the street, bore a door-plate with the name Dr. Rufus Mulbridge, and Libby drew up in front of it without having had to alarm the village with inquiries. Grace forbade his help in dismounting, and ran to the door, where she rang one of those bells which sharply respond at the back of the panel to the turn of a crank in front; she observed, in a difference of paint, that this modern improvement had displaced an old-fashioned knocker. The door was opened by a tall and strikingly handsome old woman, whose black eyes still kept their keen light under her white hair, and whose dress showed none of the incongruity which was offensive in the door-bell: it was in the perfection of an antiquated taste, which, however, came just short of characterizing it with gentle womanliness.

"Is Dr. Mulbridge at home?" asked Grace.

William Dean Howells

"Yes," said the other, with a certain hesitation, and holding the door ajar.

"I should like to see him," said Grace, mounting to the threshold.

"Is it important?" asked the elder woman.

"Quite," replied Grace, with an accent at once of surprise and decision.

"You may come in," said the other reluctantly, and she opened a door into a room at the side of the hall.

"You may give Dr. Mulbridge my card, if you please," said Grace, before she turned to go into this room; and the other took it, and left her to find a chair for herself. It was a country doctor's office, with the usual country doctor's supply of drugs on a shelf, but very much more than the country doctor's usual library: the standard works were there, and there were also the principal periodicals and the latest treatises of note in the medical world. In a long, upright case, like that of an old hall-clock, was the anatomy of one who had long done with time; a laryngoscope and some other professional apparatus of constant utility lay upon the leaf of the doctor's desk. There was nothing in the room which did not suggest his profession, except the sword and the spurs which hung upon the wall opposite where Grace sat beside one of the front windows. She spent her time in study of the room and its appointments, and in now and then glancing out at Mr. Libby, who sat statuesquely patient in the buggy. His profile cut against the sky was blameless; and a humorous shrewdness which showed in the wrinkle at his eye and in the droop of his yellow mustache gave its regularity life and charm. It occurred to her that if Dr. Mulbridge caught sight of Mr. Libby before he saw her, or before she could explain that she had got one of the gentlemen at the hotel - she resolved upon this prevarication - to drive her to Corbitant in default of another conveyance, he would have his impressions and conjectures, which doubtless the bunch of lilies in her hand would do their part to stimulate. She submitted to this possibility, and waited for his coming, which began to seem unreasonably delayed. The door opened at last, and a tall, powerfully framed man of thirty-five or forty, dressed in an ill-fitting suit of gray Canada homespun appeared. He moved with a slow, pondering step, and carried his shaggy head bent downwards from shoulders slightly rounded. His dark beard was already grizzled, and she saw that his mustache was burnt and turned tawny at points by smoking, of which habit his presence gave stale evidence to another sense. He held Grace's card in his hand, and he looked at her, as he advanced, out of gray eyes that, if not sympathetic, were perfectly intelligent, and that at once sought to divine and class her. She perceived that he took in the lilies and her coming color; she felt that he noted her figure and her dress.

She half rose in response to his questioning bow, and he motioned her to her seat again. "I had to keep you waiting," he said. "I was up all night with a patient, and I was asleep when my mother called me." He stopped here, and definitively waited for her to begin.

She did not find this easy, as he took a chair in front of her, and sat looking steadily in her face. "I'm sorry to have disturbed you" "Oh, not at all," he interrupted. "The rule is to disturb a doctor."

"I mean," she began again, "that I am not sure that I am justified in disturbing you."

He waited a little while for her to go on, and then he said, "Well, let us hear."

"I wish to consult with you," she broke out, and again she came to a sudden pause; and as she looked into his vigilant face, in which she was not sure there was not a hovering derision, she could not continue. She felt that she ought to gather courage from the fact that he had not started, or done

William Dean Howells

anything positively disagreeable when she had asked for a consultation; but she could not, and it did not avail her to reflect that she was rendering herself liable to all conceivable misconstruction, - that she was behaving childishly, with every appearance of behaving guiltily.

He came to her aid again, in a blunt fashion, neither kind nor unkind, but simply common sense. "What is the matter?"

"What is the matter?" she repeated.

"Yes. What are the symptoms? Where and how are, you sick?"

"I am not sick," she cried. They stared at each other in reciprocal amazement and mystification.

"Then excuse me if I ask you what you wish me to do?"

"Oh!" said Grace, realizing his natural error, with a flush. "It isn't in regard to myself that I wish to consult with you. It's another person - a friend" -

"Well," said Dr. Mulbridge, laughing, with the impatience of a physician used to making short cuts through the elaborate and reluctant statements of ladies seeking advice, "what is the matter with your friend?"

"She has been an invalid for some time," replied Grace. The laugh, which had its edge of patronage and conceit, stung her into self-possession again, and she briefly gave the points of Mrs. Maynard's case, with the recent accident and the symptoms developed during the night. He listened attentively, nodding his head at times, and now and then glancing sharply at her, as one might at a surprisingly intelligent child.

"I must see her," he said decidedly, when she came to an end. "I will see her as soon as possible. I will come over to Jocelyn's this afternoon, - as soon as I can get my dinner, in fact."

There was such a tone of dismissal in his words that she rose, and he promptly followed her example. She stood hesitating a moment. Then, "I don't know whether you understood that I wish merely to consult with you," she said; "that I don't wish to relinquish the case to you" -

"Relinquish the case - consult" - Dr. Mulbridge stared at her. "No, I don't understand. What do you mean by not relinquishing the case? If there is some one else in attendance."

"I am in attendance," said the girl firmly. "I am Mrs. Maynard's physician."

"You? Physician"

"If you have looked at my card" - she began with indignant severity.

He gave a sort of roar of amusement and apology, and then he stared at her again with much of the interest of a naturalist in an extraordinary specimen.

"I beg your pardon," he exclaimed. "I didn't look at it"; but he now did so, where he held it crumpled in the palm of his left hand. "My mother said it was a young lady, and I didn't look. Will you will you sit down, Dr. Breen?" He bustled in getting her several chairs. "I live off here in a corner, and I have never happened to meet any ladies of our profession before. Excuse me, if I spoke under a - mistaken impression. I - I - I should not have - ah - taken you for a physician. You" - He checked himself, as if he might have been going to say that she was too young and too pretty. "Of course, I shall have pleasure in consulting with you in regard to your friend's case, though I've no doubt you are doing all that can be done." With a great show of deference, he still betrayed something of the air of one who humors a joke; and she felt this, but felt that she could not openly resent it.

"Thank you," she returned with dignity, indicating with a

gesture of her hand that she would not sit down again. "I am sorry to ask you to come so far."

"Oh, not at all. I shall be driving over in that direction at any rate. I've a patient near there." He smiled upon her with frank curiosity, and seemed willing to detain her, but at a loss how to do so. "If I hadn't been stupid from my nap I should have inferred a scientific training from your statement of your friend's case." She still believed that he was laughing at her, and that this was a mock but she was still helpless to resent it, except by an assumption of yet colder state. This had apparently no effect upon Dr. Mulbridge. He continued to look at her with hardly concealed amusement, and visibly to grow more and more conscious of her elegance and style, now that she stood before him. There had been a time when, in planning her career, she had imagined herself studying a masculine simplicity and directness of address; but the over-success of some young women, her fellows at the school, in this direction had disgusted her with it, and she had perceived that after all there is nothing better for a girl, even a girl who is a doctor of medicine, than a ladylike manner. Now, however, she wished that she could do or say something aggressively mannish, for she felt herself dwindling away to the merest femininity, under a scrutiny which had its fascination, whether agreeable or disagreeable. "You must," he said, with really unwarrantable patronage, "have found that the study of medicine has its difficulties, - you must have been very strongly drawn to it."

"Oh no, not at all; I had rather an aversion at first," she replied, with the instant superiority of a woman where the man suffers any topic to become personal. "Why did you think I was drawn to it?"

"I don't know - I don't know that I thought so," he stammered. "I believe I intended to ask," he added bluntly; but she had the satisfaction of seeing him redden, and she did not volunteer anything in his relief. She divined that it would leave him with an awkward sense of defeat if he quitted the subject there; and in fact he had determined that he would not. "Some of our ladies take up the study abroad," he said; and he went on to speak, with a real deference, of the eminent woman who did the American name honor by the distinction she achieved in the schools of Paris.

"I have never been abroad," said Grace.

"No?" he exclaimed. "I thought all American ladies had been abroad"; and now he said, with easy recognition of her resolution not to help him out, "I suppose you have your diploma from the Philadelphia school."

"No," she returned, "from the New York school, - the homoeopathic school of New York."

Dr. Mulbridge instantly sobered, and even turned a little pale, but he did not say anything. He remained looking at her as if she had suddenly changed from a piquant mystery to a terrible dilemma.

She moved toward the door. "Then I may expect you," she said, "about the middle of the afternoon."

He did not reply; he stumbled upon the chairs in following her a pace or two, with a face of acute distress. Then he broke out with "I can't come! I can't consult with you!"

She turned and looked at him with astonishment, which he did his best to meet. Her astonishment congealed into hauteur, and then dissolved into the helplessness of a lady who has been offered a rudeness; but still she did not speak. She merely looked at him, while he halted and stammered on.

"Personally, I - I - should be - obliged - I should feel honored - I - I - It has nothing to do with your - your - being a - a - a - woman lady. I should not care for that. No. But surely you must know the reasons - the obstacles - which deter me?"

William Dean Howells

"No, I don't," she said, calm with the advantage of his perturbation. "But if you refuse, that is sufficient. I will not inquire your reasons. I will simply withdraw my request."

"Thank you. But I beg you to understand that they have no reference whatever to you in - your own - capacity - character - individual quality. They are purely professional - that is, technical - I should say disciplinary, - entirely disciplinary. Yes, disciplinary." The word seemed to afford Dr. Mulbridge the degree of relief which can come only from an exactly significant and luminously exegetic word.

"I don't at all know what you mean," said Grace. "But it is not necessary that I should know. Will you allow me?" she asked, for Dr. Mulbridge had got between her and the door, and stood with his hand on the latch.

His face flushed, and drops stood on his forehead. "Surely, Miss - I mean Doctor - Breen, you must know why I can't consult with you! We belong to two diametrically opposite schools - theories - of medicine. It would be impracticable - impossible for us to consult. We could find no common ground. Have you never heard that the - ah regular practice cannot meet homoeopathists in this way? If you had told me - if I had known - you were a homoeopathist, I couldn't have considered the matter at all. I can't now express any opinion as to your management of the case, but I have no doubt that you will know what to do - from your point of view - and that you will prefer to call in some one of your own - persuasion. I hope that you don't hold me personally responsible for this result!"

"Oh, no!" replied the girl, with a certain dreamy abstraction. "I had heard that you made some such distinction - I remember, now. But I couldn't realize anything so ridiculous."

Dr. Mulbridge colored. "Excuse me," he said, "if, even under the circumstances, I can't agree with you that the position taken by the regular practice is ridiculous."

She did not make any direct reply. "But I supposed that you only made this distinction, as you call it, in cases where there is no immediate danger; that in a matter of life and death you would waive it. Mrs. Maynard is really - "

"There are no conditions under which I could not conscientiously refuse to waive it."

"Then," cried Grace, "I withdraw the word! It is not ridiculous. It is monstrous, atrocious, inhuman!"

A light of humorous irony glimmered in Dr. Mulbridge's eye. "I must submit to your condemnation."

"Oh, it isn't a personal condemnation!" she retorted. "I have no doubt that personally you are not responsible. We can lay aside our distinctions as allopathist and homoeopathist, and you can advise with me" -

"It's quite impossible," said Dr. Mulbridge. "If I advised with you, I might be - A little while ago one of our school in Connecticut was expelled from the State Medical Association for consulting with" - he began to hesitate, as if he had not hit upon a fortunate or appropriate illustration, but he pushed on - "with his own wife, who was a physician of your school."

She haughtily ignored his embarrassment. "I can appreciate your difficulty, and pity any liberal-minded person who is placed as you are, and disapproves of such wretched bigotry."

"I am obliged to tell you," said Dr. Mulbridge, "that I don't disapprove of it."

"I am detaining you," said Grace. "I beg your pardon. I was curious to know how far superstition and persecution can go in our day." If the epithets were not very accurate, she used them with a woman's effectiveness, and her intention made them descriptive. "Good-day," she added, and she made a movement toward the door, from which Dr. Mulbridge retired. But she did not open the door. Instead, she sank into the chair which stood in the corner, and passed her hand over her forehead, as if she were giddy.

Dr. Mulbridge's finger was instantly on her wrist. "Are you faint?"

"No, no!" she gasped, pulling her hand away. "I am perfectly well." Then she was silent for a time before she added by a supreme effort, "I have no right to endanger another's life, through any miserable pride, and I never will. Mrs. Maynard needs greater experience than mine, and she must have it. I can't justify myself in the delay and uncertainty of sending to Boston. I relinquish the case. I give it to you. And I will nurse her under your direction, obediently, conscientiously. Oh!" she cried, at his failure to make any immediate response, "surely you won't refuse to take the case!"

"I won't refuse," he said, with an effect of difficult concession. "I will come. I will drive over at once, after dinner."

She rose now, and put her hand on the door-latch. "Do you object to my nursing your patient? She is an old school friend. But I could yield that point too, if" -

"Oh, no, no! I shall be only too glad of your help, and your" - he was going to say advice, but he stopped himself, and repeated - "help."

They stood inconclusively a moment, as if they would both be glad of something more to say. Then she said tentatively, "Good-morning," and he responded experimentally, "Good-morning"; and with that they involuntarily parted, and she went out of the door, which he stood holding open even after she had got out of the gate.

His mother came down the stairs. "What in the world were you quarrelling with that girl about, Rufus?"

"We were not quarrelling, mother."

"Well, it sounded like it. Who was she?

"Who?" repeated her son absently. "Dr. Breen."

"Doctor Breen? That girl a doctor?"

"Yes."

"I thought she was some saucy thing. Well, upon my word!" exclaimed Mrs. Mulbridge. "So that is a female doctor, is it? Was she sick?"

"No," said her son, with what she knew to be professional finality. "Mother, if you can hurry dinner a little, I shall be glad. I have to drive over to Jocelyn's, and I should like to start as soon as possible."

"Who was the young man with her? Her beau, I guess."

"Was there a young man with her?" asked Dr. Mulbridge.

His mother went out without speaking. She could be unsatisfactory, too.

VI

No one but Mrs. Breen knew of her daughter's errand, and when Grace came back she alighted from Mr. Libby's buggy with an expression of thanks that gave no clew as to the direction or purpose of it. He touched his hat to her with equal succinctness, and drove away, including all the ladies on the piazza in a cursory obeisance.

"We must ask you, Miss Gleason," said Mrs. Alger. "Your admiration of Dr. Breen clothes you with authority and responsibility."

"I can't understand it at all," Miss Gleason confessed. "But I'm sure there's nothing in it. He isn't her equal. She would feel that it wasn't right - under the circumstances."

"But if Mrs. Maynard was well it would be a fair game, you mean," said Mrs. Alger.

"No," returned Miss Gleason, with the greatest air of candor, "I can't admit that I meant that."

"Well," said the elder lady, "the presumption is against them. Every young couple seen together must be considered in love till they prove the contrary."

"I like it in her," said Mrs. Frost. "It shows that she is human, after all. It shows that she is like other girls. It's a relief."

"She isn't like other girls," contended Miss Gleason darkly.

"I would rather have Mr. Libby's opinion," said Mrs. Merritt.

Grace went to Mrs. Maynard's room, and told her that Dr. Mulbridge was coming directly after dinner.

"I knew you would do it!" cried Mrs. Maynard, throwing her right arm round Grace's neck, while the latter bent over to feel the pulse in her left. "I knew where you had gone as soon as your mother told me you had driven off with Walter Libby. I'm so glad that you've got somebody to consult! Your theories are perfectly right and I'm sure that Dr. Mulbridge will just tell you to keep on as you've been doing."

Grace withdrew from her caress. "Dr. Mulbridge is not coming for a consultation. He refused to consult with me."

"Refused to consult? Why, how perfectly ungentlemanly! Why did he refuse?"

"Because he is an allopathist and I am a homoeopathist."

"Then, what is he coming for, I should like to know!"

"I have given up the case to him," said Grace wearily.

"Very well, then!" cried Mrs. Maynard, "I won't be given up. I will simply die! Not a pill, not a powder, of his will I touch! If he thinks himself too good to consult with another doctor, and a lady at that, merely because she doesn't happen to be allopathist, he can go along! I never heard of anything so conceited, so disgustingly mean, in my life. No, Grace! Why, it's horrid!" She was silent, and then, "Why, of course," she added, "if he comes, I shall have to see him. I look like a fright, I suppose."

"I will do your hair," said Grace, with indifference to these vows and protests; and without deigning further explanation or argument she made the invalid's toilet for her. If given time, Mrs. Maynard would talk herself into any necessary frame of mind, and Grace merely supplied the monosyllabic promptings requisite for her transition from mood to mood. It was her final resolution that when Dr. Mulbridge did come she should give him a piece of her mind; and she received him with anxious submissiveness, and hung upon all his looks and words with quaking and with an inclination to attribute her unfavorable symptoms to the treatment of her former physician. She did not spare him certain apologies for the disorderly appearance of her person and her room.

Grace sat by and watched him with perfectly quiescent observance. The large, somewhat uncouth man gave evidence to her intelligence that he was all physician - that he had not chosen his profession from any theory or motive, however good, but had been as much chosen by it as if he had been born a Physician. He was incredibly gentle and soft in all his movements, and perfectly kind, without being at any moment unprofitably sympathetic. He knew when to listen and when not to listen, - to learn everything from the quivering bundle of nerves before him without seeming to have learnt anything alarming; he smiled when it would do her good to be laughed at, and treated her with such grave respect that she could not feel herself trifled with, nor remember afterwards any point of neglect. When he rose and left some medicines, with directions to Grace for giving them and instructions for contingencies, she followed him from the room.

"Well?" she said anxiously.

"Mrs. Maynard is threatened with pneumonia. Or, I don't know why I should say threatened," he added; "she has pneumonia."

"I supposed - I was afraid so," faltered the girl.

"Yes." He looked into her eyes with even more seriousness than he spoke.

"Has she friends here?" he asked.

"No; her husband is in Cheyenne, out on the plains."

"He ought to know," said Dr. Mulbridge. "A great deal will depend upon her nursing - Miss - ah - Dr. Breen."

"You needn't call me Dr. Breen," said Grace. "At present, I am Mrs. Maynard's nurse."

He ignored this as he had ignored every point connected with the interview of the morning. He repeated the directions he had already given with still greater distinctness, and, saying that he should come in the morning, drove away. She went back to Louise: inquisition for inquisition, it was easier to meet that of her late patient than that of her mother, and for once the girl spared herself.

"I know he thought I was very bad," whimpered Mrs. Maynard, for a beginning. "What is the matter with me?"

"Your cold has taken an acute form; you will have to go to bed."

"Then I 'm going to be down sick! I knew I was! I knew it! And what am I going to do, off in such a place as this? No one to nurse me, or look after Bella! I should think you would be satisfied now, Grace, with the result of your conscientiousness: you were so very sure that Mr. Libby was wanting to flirt with me that you drove us to our death, because you thought he felt guilty and was trying to fib out of it."

"Will you let me help to undress you?" asked Grace gently. "Bella shall be well taken care of, and I am going to nurse you myself, under Dr. Mulbridge's direction. And once for all, Louise, I wish to say that I hold myself to blame for all" -

"Oh, yes! Much good that does now!" Being got into bed, with the sheet smoothed under her chin, she said, with the effect of

William Dean Howells

drawing a strictly logical conclusion from the premises, "Well, I should think George Maynard would want to be with his family!"

Spent with this ordeal, Grace left her at last, and went out on the piazza, where she found Libby returned. In fact, he had, upon second thoughts, driven back, and put up his horse at Jocelyn's, that he might be of service there in case he were needed. The ladies, with whom he had been making friends, discreetly left him to Grace, when she appeared, and she frankly walked apart with him, and asked him if he could go over to New Leyden, and telegraph to Mr. Maynard.

"Has she asked for him?" he inquired, laughing. "I knew it would come to that."

"She has not asked; she has said that she thought he ought to be with his family," repeated Grace faithfully.

"Oh, I know how she said it: as if he had gone away wilfully, and kept away against her wishes and all the claims of honor and duty. It wouldn't take her long to get round to that if she thought she was very sick. Is she so bad?" he inquired, with light scepticism.

"She's threatened with pneumonia. We can't tell how bad she may be."

"Why, of course I'll telegraph. But I don't think anything serious can be the matter with Mrs. Maynard."

"Dr. Mulbridge said that Mr. Maynard ought to know."

"Is that so?" asked Libby, in quite a different tone. If she recognized the difference, she was meekly far from resenting it; he, however, must have wished to repair his blunder. "I think you needn't have given up the case to him. I think you're too conscientious about it."

"Please don't speak of that now," she interposed.

"Well, I won't," he consented. "Can I be of any use here to-night?"

"No, we shall need nothing more. The doctor will be here again in the morning."

"Libby did not come in the morning till after the doctor had gone, and then he explained that he had waited to hear in reply to his telegram, so that they might tell Mrs. Maynard her husband had started; and he had only just now heard.

"And has he started?" Grace asked.

"I heard from his partner. Maynard was at the ranch. His partner had gone for him."

"Then he will soon be here," she said.

"He will, if telegraphing can bring him. I sat up half the night with the operator. She was very obliging when she understood the case."

"She?" reputed Grace, with a slight frown.

"The operators are nearly all women in the country."

"Oh!" She looked grave. "Can they trust young girls with such important duties?"

"They didn't in this instance," relied Libby. "She was a pretty old girl. What made you think she was young?"

"I don't know. I thought you said she was young." She blushed, and seemed about to say more, but she did not.

He waited, and then he said, "You can tell Mrs. Maynard that I telegraphed on my own responsibility, if you think it's going to alarm her."

"Well," said Grace, with a helpless sigh.

"You don't like to tell her that," he suggested, after a moment, in which he had watched her.

"How do you know?"

"Oh, I know. And some day I will tell you how - if you will let me."

It seemed a question; and she did not know what it was that kept her - silent and breathless and hot in the throat. "I don't like to do it," she said at last. "I hate myself whenever I have to feign anything. I knew perfectly well that you didn't say she was young," she broke out desperately.

"Say Mrs. Maynard was young?" he asked stupidly.

"No!" she cried. She rose hastily from the bench where she had been sitting with him. "I must go back to her now."

He mounted to his buggy, and drove thoughtfully away at a walk.

The ladies, whose excited sympathies for Mrs. Maynard had kept them from the beach till now, watched him quite out of sight before they began to talk of Grace.

"I hope Dr. Breen's new patient will be more tractable," said Mrs. Merritt. "It would be a pity if she had to give him up, too, to Dr. Mulbridge."

Mrs. Scott failed of the point. "Why, is Mr. Libby sick?"

"Not very," answered Mrs. Merritt, with a titter of self-applause.

"I should be sorry," interposed Mrs. Alger authoritatively, "if we had said anything to influence the poor thing in what she has done."

"Oh, I don't think we need distress ourselves about undue influence!" Mrs. Merritt exclaimed.

Mrs. Alger chose to ignore the suggestion. "She had a very difficult part; and I think she has acted courageously. I always feel sorry for girls who attempt anything of that kind. It's a fearful ordeal."

"But they say Miss Breen wasn't obliged to do it for a living," Mrs. Scott suggested.

"So much the worse," said Mrs. Merritt.

"No, so much the better," returned Mrs. Alger.

Mrs. Merritt, sitting on the edge of the piazza, stooped over with difficulty and plucked a glass-straw, which she bit as she looked rebelliously away.

Mrs. Frost had installed herself as favorite since Mrs. Alger had praised her hair. She now came forward, and, dropping fondly at her knee, looked up to her for instruction. "Don't you think that she showed her sense in giving up at the very beginning, if she found she wasn't equal to it?" She gave her head a little movement from side to side, and put the mass of her back hair more on show.

"Perhaps," said Mrs. Alger, looking at the favorite not very favorably.

"Oh, I don't think she's given up," Miss Gleason interposed, in her breathless manner. She waited to be asked why, and then she added, "I think she's acting in consultation with Dr. Mulbridge. He may have a certain influence over her, - I think he has; but I know they are acting in unison."

Mrs. Merritt flung her grass-straw away. "Perhaps it is to be Dr. Mulbridge, after all, and not Mr. Libby."

"I have thought of that," Miss Gleason assented candidly. "Yes, I have thought of that. I have thought of their being constantly thrown together, in this way. It would not discourage me. She could be quite as true to her vocation as if she remained single. Truer."

"Talking of true," said Mrs. Scott, "always does make me think of blue. They say that yellow will be worn on everything this winter."

"Old gold?" asked Mrs. Frost. "Yes, more than ever."

"Dear!" cried the other lady. "I don't know what I shall do. It perfectly kills my hair."

"Oh, Miss Gleason!" exclaimed the young girl.

"Do you believe in character coming out in color?"

"Yes, certainly. I have always believed that."

"Well, I've got a friend, and she wouldn't have anything to do with a girl that wore magenta more than she would fly."

"I should suppose," explained Miss Gleason, "that all those aniline dyes implied something coarse in people."

"Isn't it curious," asked Mrs. Frost, "how red-haired people have come in fashion? I can recollect, when I was a little girl, that everybody laughed at red hair. There was one girl at the first school I ever went to, - the boys used to pretend to burn their fingers at her hair."

"I think Dr. Breen's hair is a very pretty shade of brown," said the young girl.

Mrs. Merritt rose from the edge of the piazza. "I think that if she hasn't given up to him entirely she's the most submissive consulting physician I ever saw," she said, and walked out over the grass towards the cliff.

The ladies looked after her. "Is Mrs. Merritt more pudgy when she's sitting down or when she's standing up?" asked Mrs. Scott.

Miss Gleason seized her first chance of speaking with Grace alone. "Oh, do you know how much you are doing for us all?"

"Doing for you, all? How doing?" faltered Grace, whom she had whisperingly halted in a corner of the hall leading from the dining-room.

"By acting in unison, - by solving the most perplexing problem in women's practising your profession. She passed the edge of her fan over her lips before letting it fall furled upon her left hand, and looked luminously into Grace's eyes.

"I don't at all know what you mean, Miss Gleason," said the other.

Miss Gleason kicked out the skirt of her dress, so as to leave herself perfectly free for the explanation. "Practising in harmony with a physician of the other sex. I have always felt that there was the great difficulty, - how to bring that about. I have always felt that the TRUE physician must be DUAL, - have both the woman's nature and the man's; the woman's tender touch, the man's firm grasp. You have shown how the medical education of women can meet this want. The physician can actually be dual, - be two, in fact. Hereafter, I have no doubt we shall always call a physician of each sex. But it's wonderful how you could ever bring it about, though you can do anything! Hasn't it worn upon you?" Miss Gleason darted out her sentences in quick, short breaths, fixing Grace with her eyes, and at each clause nervously tapping her chest with her reopened fan.

William Dean Howells

"If you suppose," said Grace, "that Dr. Mulbridge and I are acting professionally in unison, as you call it, you are mistaken. He has entire charge of the case; I gave it up to him, and I am merely nursing Mrs. Maynard under his direction."

"How splendid!" Miss Gleason exclaimed. "Do you know that I admire you for giving up, - for knowing when to give up? So few women do that! Isn't he magnificent?"

"Magnificent?"

"I mean psychically. He is what I should call a strong soul You must have felt his masterfulness; you must have enjoyed it! Don't you like to be dominated?"

"No," said Grace, "I shouldn't at all like it."

"Oh, I do! I like to meet one of those forceful masculine natures that simply bid you obey. It's delicious. Such a sense of self-surrender," Miss Gleason explained. "It isn't because they are men," she added. "I have felt the same influence from some women. I felt it, in a certain degree, on first meeting you."

"I am very sorry," said Grace coldly. "I should dislike being controlled
myself, and I should dislike still more to control others."

"You're doing it now!" cried Miss Gleason, with delight. "I could not do a thing to resist your putting me down! Of course you don't know that you're doing it; it's purely involuntary. And you wouldn't know that he was dominating you. And he wouldn't."

Very probably Dr. Mulbridge would not have recognized himself in the character of all-compelling lady's-novel hero, which Miss Gleason imagined for him. Life presented itself rather simply to him, as it does to most men, and he easily dismissed its subtler problems from a mind preoccupied with active cares. As far as Grace was concerned, she had certainly roused in him an unusual curiosity; nothing less than her homoeopathy would have made him withdraw his consent to a consultation with her, and his fear had been that in his refusal she should escape from his desire to know more about her, her motives, her purposes. He had accepted without scruple the sacrifice of pride she had made to him; but he had known how to appreciate her scientific training, which he found as respectable as that of any clever, young man of their profession. He praised, in his way, the perfection with which she interpreted his actions and intentions in regard to the patient. "If there were such nurses as you, Miss Breen, there would be very little need of doctors," he said, with a sort of interogative fashion of laughing peculiar to him.

"I thought of being a nurse once;" she answered. "Perhaps I may still be one. The scientific training won't be lost."

"Oh, no? It's a pity that more of them haven't it. But I suppose they think nursing is rather too humble an ambition."

"I don't think it so," said Grace briefly.

"Then you didn't care for medical distinction."

"No."

He looked at her quizzically, as if this were much droller than if she had cared. "I don't understand why you should have gone into it. You told me, I think, that it was repugnant to you; and it's hard work for a woman, and very uncertain work for anyone. You must have had a tremendous desire to benefit your race."

His characterization of her motive was so distasteful that she made no reply, and left him to his conjectures, in which he did not appear unhappy. "How do you find Mrs. Maynard to-day?" she asked.

He looked at her with an instant coldness, as if he did not like her asking, and were hesitating whether to answer. But he said at last, "She is no better. She will be worse before she is better. You see," he added, "that I haven't been able to arrest the disorder in its first stage. We must hope for what can be done now, in the second."

She had gathered from the half jocose ease with which he had listened to Mrs. Maynard's account of herself, and to her own report, an encouragement which now fell to the ground "Yes," she assented, in her despair, "that is the only hope."

He sat beside the table in the hotel parlor, where they found themselves alone for the moment, and drubbed upon it with an absent look. "Have you sent for her husband?" he inquired, returning to himself.

"Yes; Mr. Libby telegraphed the evening we saw you."

"That's good," said Dr. Mulbridge, with comfortable approval; and he rose to go away.

Grace impulsively detained him. "I - won't - ask you whether you consider Mrs. Maynard's case a serious one, if you object to my doing so."

"I don't know that I object," he said slowly, with a teasing smile, such as one might use with a persistent child whom one chose to baffle in that way.

She disdained to avail herself of the implied permission. "What I mean - what I wish to tell you is - that I feel myself responsible for her sickness, and that if she dies, I shall be guilty of her death."

"Ah?" said Dr. Mulbridge, with more interest, but the same smile. "What do you mean?"

"She didn't wish to go that day when she was caught in the storm. But I insisted; I forced her to go." She stood panting with the intensity of the feeling which had impelled her utterance.

"What do you mean by forcing her to go?"

"I don't know. I - I - persuaded her."

Dr. Mulbridge smiled, as if he perceived her intention not to tell him something she wished to tell him. He looked down into his hat, which he carried in his hand.

"Did you believe the storm was coming?"

"No!"

"And you didn't make it come?"

"Of course not!"

He looked at her and laughed.

"Oh, you don't at all understand!" she cried.

"I'm not a doctor of divinity," he said. "Good morning."

"Wait, wait!" she implored, "I'm afraid - I don't know - Perhaps my being near her is injurious to her; perhaps I ought to let some one else nurse her. I wished to ask you this" - She stopped breathlessly.

"I don't think you have done her any harm as yet," he answered lightly.

"However," he said, after a moment's consideration, "why don't you take a holiday? Some of the other ladies might look after her a while."

"Do you really think," she palpitated, "that I might? Do you think I ought? I'm afraid I oughtn't" -

"Not if your devotion is hurtful to her?" he asked. "Send some one else to her for a while. Any one can take care of her for a few hours."

"I couldn't leave her - feeling as I do about her."

"I don't know how you feel about her," said Dr. Mulbridge. "But you can't go on at this rate. I shall want your help by and by, and Mrs. Maynard doesn't need you now. Don't go back to her."

"But if she should get worse while I am away" -

"You think your staying and feeling bad would make her better? Don't go back," he repeated; and he went out to his ugly rawboned horse, and, mounting his shabby wagon, rattled away. She lingered, indescribably put to shame by the brutal common sense which she could not impeach, but which she still felt was no measure of the case. It was true that she had not told him everything, and she could not complain that he had mocked her appeal for sympathy if she had trifled with him by a partial confession. But she indignantly denied to herself that she had wished to appeal to him for sympathy.

She wandered out on the piazza, which she found empty, and stood gazing at the sea in a revery of passionate humiliation. She was in that mood, familiar to us all, when we long to be consoled and even flattered for having been silly. In a woman this mood is near to tears; at a touch of kindness the tears come, and momentous questions are decided. What was perhaps uppermost in the girl's heart was a detestation of the man to whom she had seemed a simpleton; her thoughts pursued him, and divined the contempt with which he must be thinking of her and her pretensions. She heard steps on the sand, and Libby came round the corner of the house from the stable.

VII

Libby's friends had broken up their camp on the beach, and had gone to a lake in the heart of the woods for the fishing. He had taken a room at the Long Beach House, but he spent most of his time at Jocelyn's, where he kept his mare for use in going upon errands for Mrs. Maynard. Grace saw him constantly, and he was always doing little things for her with a divination of her unexpressed desires which women find too rarely in men. He brought her flowers, which, after refusing them for Mrs. Maynard the first time, she accepted for herself. He sometimes brought her books, the light sort which form the sentimental currency of young people, and she lent them round among the other ladies, who were insatiable of them. She took a pleasure in these attentions, as if they had been for some one else. In this alien sense she liked to be followed up with a chair to the point where she wished to sit; to have her hat fetched, or her shawl; to drop her work or her handkerchief, secure that it would be picked up for her.

It all interested her, and it was a relief from the circumstances that would have forbidden her to recognize it as gallantry, even if her own mind had not been so far from all thought of that. His kindness followed often upon some application of hers for his advice or help, for she had fallen into the habit of going to him with difficulties. He had a prompt common sense that made him very useful in emergencies, and a sympathy or an insight that was quick in suggestions and expedients. Perhaps she overrated other qualities of his in her admiration of the practical readiness which kept his amiability from seeming

William Dean Howells

weak. But the practical had so often been the unattainable with her that it was not strange she should overrate it, and that she should rest upon it in him with a trust that included all he chose to do in her behalf.

"What is the matter, Mr. Libby?" she asked, as he came toward her.

"Is anything the matter?" he demanded in turn.

"Yes; you are looking downcast," she cried reproachfully.

"I didn't know that I mustn't look downcast. I didn't suppose it would be very polite, under the circumstances, to go round looking as bobbish as I feel."

"It's the best thing you could possibly do. But you're not feeling very bobbish now." A woman respects the word a man uses, not because she would have chosen it, but because she thinks that he has an exact intention in it, which could not be reconveyed in a more feminine phrase. In this way slang arises. "Isn't it time for Mr. Maynard to be here?"

"Yes," he answered. Then, "How did you know I was thinking of that?"

"I didn't. I only happened to think it was time. What are you keeping back, Mr. Libby?" she pursued tremulously.

"Nothing, upon my honor. I almost wish there were something to keep back. But there isn't anything. There haven't been any accidents reported. And I shouldn't keep anything back from you."

"Why?"

"Because you would be equal to it, whatever it was."

"I don't see why you say that." She weakly found comfort in

the praise which she might once have resented as patronage.

"I don't see why I shouldn't," he retorted:

"Because I am not fit to be trusted at all."

"Do you mean" -

"Oh, I haven't the strength, to mean anything," she said. "But I thank you, thank you very much," she added. She turned her head away.

"Confound Maynard!" cried the young man. "I don't see why he doesn't come. He must have started four days ago. He ought to have' had sense enough to telegraph when he did start. I didn't tell his partner to ask him. You can't think of everything. I've been trying to find out something. I'm going over to Leyden, now, to try to wake up somebody in Cheyenne who knows Maynard." He looked ruefully at Grace, who listened with anxious unintelligence. "You're getting worn out, Miss Breen," he said. "I wish I could ask you to go with me to Leyden. It would do you good. But my mare's fallen lame; I've just been to see her. Is there anything I can do for you over there?"

"Why, how are you going?" she asked.

"In my boat," he answered consciously.

"The same boat?"

"Yes. I've had her put to rights. She wasn't much damaged."

She was silent a moment, while he stood looking down at her in the chair into which she had sunk. "Does it take you long?"

"Oh, no. It's shorter than it is by land. I shall have the tide with me both ways. I can make the run there and back in a couple of hours."

"Two hours?"

"Yes."

A sudden impulse, unreasoned and unreasonable, in which there seemed hope of some such atonement, or expiation, as the same ascetic nature would once have found in fasting or the scourge, prevailed with her. She rose. "Mr. Libby," she panted, "if you will let me, I should like to go with you in your boat. Do you think it will be rough?"

"No, it's a light breeze; just right. You needn't be afraid."

"I'm not afraid. I should not care if it were rough! I should not care if it stormed! I hope it - I will ask mother to stay with Mrs. Maynard."

Mrs. Breen had not been pleased to have her daughter in charge of Mrs. Maynard's case, but she had not liked her giving it up. She had said more than once that she had no faith in Dr. Mulbridge. She willingly consented to Grace's prayer, and went down into Mrs. Maynard's room, and insinuated misgivings in which the sick woman found so much reason that they began for the first time to recognize each other's good qualities. They decided that the treatment was not sufficiently active, and that she should either have something that would be more loosening to the cough, or some application - like mustard plasters - to her feet, so as to take away that stuffed feeling about the head.

At that hour of the afternoon, when most of the ladies were lying down in their rooms, Grace met no one on the beach but Miss Gleason and Mrs. Alger, who rose from their beds of sand under the cliff at her passage with Mr. Libby to his dory.

"Don't you want to go to Leyden?" he asked jocosely over his shoulder.

"You don't mean to say you're going?" Miss Gleason

demanded of Grace.

"Yes, certainly. Why not?"

"Well, you are brave!"

She shut her novel upon her thumb, that she might have nothing to do but admire Grace's courage, as the girl walked away.

"It will do her good, poor thing," said the elder woman. "She looks wretchedly."

"I can understand just why she does it," murmured Miss Gleason in adoring rapture.

"I hope she does it for pleasure," said Mrs. Alger.

"It isn't that," returned Miss Gleason mysteriously.

"At any rate, Mr. Libby seemed pleased."

"Oh, she would never marry HIM!" said Miss Gleason.

The other laughed, and at that moment Grace also laughed. The strong current of her purpose, the sense of escape from the bitter servitude of the past week, and the wild hope of final expiation through the chances she was tempting gave her a buoyancy long unfelt. She laughed in gayety of heart as she helped the young man draw his dory down the sand, and then took her place at one end while he gave it the last push and then leaped in at the other. He pulled out to where the boat lay tilting at anchor, and held the dory alongside by the gunwale that she might step aboard. But after rising she faltered, looking intently at the boat as if she missed something there.

"I thought you had a man to sail your boat"

William Dean Howells

"I had. But I let him go last week. Perhaps I ought to have told you," he said, looking up at her aslant. "Are you afraid to trust my seamanship? Adams was a mere form. He behaved like a fool that day."

"Oh, I'm not afraid," said Grace. She stepped from the dory into the boat, and he flung out the dory's anchor and followed. The sail went up with a pleasant clucking of the tackle, and the light wind filled it. Libby made the sheet fast, and, sitting down in the stern on the other side, took the tiller and headed the boat toward the town that shimmered in the distance. The water hissed at the bow, and seethed and sparkled from the stern; the land breeze that bent their sail blew cool upon her cheek and freshened it with a tinge of color.

"This will do you good," he said, looking into hers with his kind, gay eyes.

The color in her cheeks deepened a little. "Oh, I am better than I look. I didn't come for" -

"For medicinal purposes. Well, I am glad of it. We've a good hour between us and news or no news from Maynard, and I should like to think we were out for pleasure. You don't object?"

"No. You can even smoke, if that will heighten the illusion."

"It will make it reality. But you don't mean it?"

"Yes; why not?"

"I don't know. But I couldn't have dreamt of smoking in your presence. And we take the liberty to dream very strange things."

"Yes," she said, "it's shocking what things we do dream of people. But am I so forbidding?" she asked, a little sadly.

"Not now," said Libby. He got out a pouch of tobacco and some cigarette papers, and putting the tiller under his arm, he made himself a cigarette.

"You seem interested," he said, as he lifted his eyes from his work, on which he found her intent, and struck his fusee.

"I was admiring your skill," she answered.

"Do you think it was worth a voyage to South America?"

"I shouldn't have thought the voyage was necessary."

"Oh, perhaps you think you can do it," he said, handing her the tobacco and papers. She took them and made a cigarette. "It took me a whole day to learn to make bad ones, and this, is beautiful. But I will never smoke it. I will keep this always."

"You had better smoke it, if you want more," she said.

"Will you make some more? I can't smoke the first one!"

"Then smoke the last," she said, offering him the things back.

"No, go on. I'll smoke it."

She lent herself to the idle humor of the time, and went on making cigarettes till there were no more papers. From time to time she looked up from this labor, and scanned the beautiful bay, which they had almost wholly to themselves. They passed a collier lagging in the deep channel, and signalling for a pilot to take her up to the town. A yacht, trim and swift, cut across their course; the ladies on board waved a salutation with their handkerchiefs, and Libby responded.

"Do you know them?" asked Grace.

"No!" he laughed. "But ladies like to take these liberties at a safe distance."

"Yes, that's a specimen of woman's daring," she said, with a self-scornful curl of the lip, which presently softened into a wistful smile. "How lovely it all is!" she sighed.

"Yes, there's nothing better in all the world than a sail. It is all the world while it lasts. A boat's like your own fireside for snugness."

A dreamier light came into her eye, which wandered, with a turn of the head giving him the tender curve of her cheek, over the levels of the bay, roughened everywhere by the breeze, but yellowish green in the channels and dark with the thick growth of eel-grass in the shallows; then she lifted her face to the pale blue heavens in an effort that slanted towards him the soft round of her chin, and showed her full throat.

"This is the kind of afternoon," she said, still looking at the sky, "that you think will never end."

"I wish it wouldn't," he answered.

She lowered her eyes to his, and asked: "Do you have times when you are sorry that you ever tried to do anything - when it seems foolish to have tried?"

"I have the other kind of times, - when I wish that I had tried to do something."

"Oh yes, I have those, too. It's wholesome to be ashamed of not having tried to do anything; but to be ashamed of having tried - it's like death. There seems no recovery from that."

He did not take advantage of her confession, or try to tempt her to further confidence; and women like men who have this wisdom, or this instinctive generosity, and trust them further.

"And the worst of it is that you can't go back and be like those that have never tried at all. If you could, that would be some consolation for having failed. There is nothing left of you but your mistake."

"Well," he said, "some people are not even mistakes. I suppose that almost any sort of success looks a good deal like failure from the inside. It must be a poor creature that comes up to his own mark. The best way is not to have any mark, and then you're in no danger of not coming up to it." He laughed, but she smiled sadly.

"You don't believe in thinking about yourself," she said.

"Oh, I try a little introspection, now and then. But I soon get through: there isn't much of me to think about."

"No, don't talk in that way," she pleaded, and she was very charming in her earnestness: it was there that her charm lay. "I want you to be serious with me, and tell me - tell me how men feel when." -

A sudden splashing startled her, and looking round she saw a multitude of curious, great-eyed, black heads, something like the heads of boys, and something like the heads of dogs, thrusting from the water, and flashing under it again at sight of them with a swish that sent the spray into the air. She sprang to her feet. "Oh, look at those things! Look at them! Look at them!" She laid vehement hands upon the young man, and pushed him in the direction in which she wished him to look, at some risk of pushing him overboard, while he laughed at her ecstasy.

"They're seals. The bay's full of them. Did you never see them on the reef at Jocelyn's?"

"I never saw them before!" she cried. "How wonderful they are! Oh!" she shouted; as one of them glanced sadly at her over its shoulder, and then vanished with a whirl of the head. "The Beatrice Cenci attitude!"

"They're always trying that," said Libby. "Look yonder." He

William Dean Howells

pointed to a bank of mud which the tide had not yet covered, and where a herd of seals lay basking in the sun. They started at his voice, and wriggling and twisting and bumping themselves over the earth to the water's edge, they plunged in. "Their walk isn't so graceful as their swim. Would you like one for a pet, Miss Breen? That's all they're good for since kerosene came in. They can't compete with that, and they're not the kind that wear the cloaks."

She was standing with her hand pressed hard upon his shoulder.

"Did they ever kill them?"

"They used to take that precaution."

"With those eyes? It was murder!" She withdrew her hand and sat down.

"Well, they only catch them, now. I tried it myself once. I set out at low tide, about ten o'clock, one night, and got between the water and the biggest seal on the bank. We fought it out on that line till daylight."

"And did you get it?" she demanded, absurdly interested.

"No, it got me. The tide came in, and the seal beat."

"I am glad of that."

"Thank you."

"What did you want with it?"

"I don't think I wanted it at all. At any rate, that's what I always said. I shall have to ask you to sit on this side," he added, loosening the sheet and preparing to shift the sail. "The wind has backed round a little more to the south, and it's getting lighter."

"If it's going down we shall be late," she said, with an intimation of apprehension.

"We shall be at Leyden on time. If the wind falls then, I can get a horse at the stable and have you driven back."

"Well."

He kept scanning the sky. Then, "Did you ever hear them whistle for a wind?" he asked.

"No. What is it like?"

"When Adams does it, it's like this." He put on a furtive look, and glanced once or twice at her askance. "Well!" he said with the reproduction of a strong nasal, "of course I don't believe there's anything in it. Of course it's all foolishness. Now you must urge me a little," he added, in his own manner.

"Oh, by all means go on, Mr. Adams," she cried, with a laugh.

He rolled his head again to one side sheepishly.

"Well, I don't presume it DOES have anything to do with the wind - well, I don't PRESUME it does." He was silent long enough to whet an imagined expectation; then he set his face towards the sky, and began a soft, low, coaxing sibilation between his teeth. "S-s-s-s; s-s-s-s-s-s! Well, it don't stand to reason it can bring the wind - S-s-s-s-s-s-s; s-s-s-s. Why, of course it's all foolishness. S-s-s-s." He continued to emit these sibilants, interspersing them with Adams's protests. Suddenly the sail pulled the loose sheet taut and the boat leaped forward over the water.

"Wonderful!" cried the girl.

"That's what I said to Adams, or words to that effect. But I thought we should get it from the look of the sky before I proposed to whistle for it. Now, then," he continued, "I will be serious, if you like."

"Serious?"

"Yes. Didn't you ask me to be serious just before those seals interrupted you?"

"Oh!" she exclaimed, coloring a little. "I don't think we can go back to that, now." He did not insist, and she said presently, "I thought the sailors had a superstition about ships that are lucky and unlucky. But you've kept your boat."

"I kept her for luck: the lightning never strikes twice in the same place. And I never saw a boat that behaved so well."

"Do you call it behaving well to tip over?"

"She behaved well before that. She didn't tip over outside the reef"

"It certainly goes very smoothly," said the girl. She had in vain recurred to the tragic motive of her coming; she could not revive it; there had been nothing like expiation in this eventless voyage; it had been a pleasure and no penance. She abandoned herself with a weak luxury to the respite from suffering and anxiety; she made herself the good comrade of the young man whom perhaps she even tempted to flatter her farther and farther out of the dreariness in which she had dwelt; and if any woful current of feeling swept beneath, she would not fathom it, but resolutely floated, as one may at such times, on the surface. They laughed together and jested; they talked in the gay idleness of such rare moods.

They passed a yacht at anchor, and a young fellow in a white duck cap, leaning over the rail, saluted Libby with the significant gravity which one young man uses towards another whom he sees in a sail-boat with a pretty girl.

She laughed at this. "Do you know your friend?" she asked.

"Yes. This time I do?"

"He fancies you are taking some young lady a sail. What would he say if you were to stop and introduce me to him as Dr. Breen?"

"Oh, he knows who you are. It's Johnson."

"The one whose clothes you came over in, that morning?"

"Yes. I suppose you laughed at me."

"I liked your having the courage to do it. But how does he know me?"

"I - I described you. He's rather an old friend." This also amused her. "I should like to hear how you described me."

"I will tell you sometime. It was an elaborate description. I couldn't get through with it now before we landed."

The old town had come out of the haze of the distance, - a straggling village of weather-beaten wood and weather-beaten white paint, picturesque, but no longer a vision of gray stone and pale marble. A coal-yard, and a brick locomotive house, and rambling railroad sheds stretched along the water-front. They found their way easily enough through the sparse shipping to the steps at the end of the wooden pier, where Libby dropped the sail and made his boat fast.

A little pleasant giddiness, as if the lightness of her heart had mounted to her head, made her glad of his arm up these steps and up the wharf; and she kept it as they climbed the sloping elm-shaded village street to the main thoroughfare, with its brick sidewalks, its shops and awnings, and its cheerful stir and traffic.

The telegraph office fronted the head of the street which they had ascended. "You can sit here in the apothecary's till I come

William Dean Howells

down," he said.

"Do you think that will be professionally appropriate? I am only a nurse now."

"No, I wasn't thinking of that. But I saw a chair in there. And we can make a pretense of wanting some soda. It is the proper thing to treat young ladies to soda when one brings them in from the country."

"It does have that appearance," she assented, with a smile. She kept him waiting with what would have looked like coquettish hesitation in another, while she glanced at the windows overhead, pierced by a skein of converging wires. "Suppose I go up with you?"

"I should like that better," he said; and she followed him lightly up the stairs that led to the telegraph office. A young man stood at the machine with a cigar in his mouth, and his eyes intent upon the ribbon of paper unreeling itself before him.

"Just hold on," he said to Libby, without turning his head. "I've got something here for you." He read: "Despatch received yesterday. Coming right through. George Maynard."

"Good!" cried Libby.

"Dated Council Bluffs. Want it written out?"

"No. What's to pay?"

"Paid," said the operator.

The laconically transacted business ended with this, the wire began to cluck again like the anxious hen whose manner the most awful and mysterious of the elements assumes in becoming articulate, and nothing remained for them but to come away.

"That was what I was afraid of," said Libby. "Maynard was at his ranch, and it must have been a good way out. They're fifty or sixty miles out, sometimes. That would account for the delay. Well, Mrs. Maynard doesn't know how long it takes to come from Cheyenne, and we can tell her he's on the way, and has telegraphed." They were walking rapidly down the street to the wharf where his boat lay. "Oh!" he exclaimed, halting abruptly. "I promised to send you back by land, if you preferred."

"Has the wind fallen?"

"Oh, no. We shall have a good breeze:"

"I won't put you to the trouble of getting a horse. I can go back perfectly well in the boat."

"Well, that's what I think," he said cheerily.

She did not respond, and he could not be aware that any change had come over her mood. But when they were once more seated in the boat, and the sail was pulling in the fresh breeze, she turned to him with a scarcely concealed indignation. "Have you a fancy for experimenting upon people, Mr. Libby?"

"Experimenting? I? I don't know in the least what you mean!"

"Why did you tell me that the operator was a woman?"

"Because the other operator is," he answered.

"Oh!" she said, and fell blankly silent.

"There is a good deal of business there. They have to have two operators," he explained, after a pause.

"Why, of course," she murmured in deep humiliation. If he had suffered her to be silent as long as she would, she might

William Dean Howells

have offered him some reparation; but he spoke.

"Why did you think I had been experimenting on you?" he asked.

"Why?" she repeated. The sense of having put herself in the wrong exasperated her with him. "Oh, I dare say you were curious. Don't you suppose I have noticed that men are puzzled at me? What did you mean by saying that you thought I would be equal to anything?"

"I meant - I thought you would like to be treated frankly."

"And you wouldn't treat everybody so?"

"I wouldn't treat Mrs. Maynard so."

"Oh!" she said. "You treat me upon a theory."

"Don't you like that? We treat everybody upon a theory" -

"Yes, I know"

"And I should tell you the worst of anything at once, because I think you are one of the kind that don't like to have their conclusions made for them."

"And you would really let women make their own conclusions," she said. "You are very peculiar!" She waited a while, and then she asked, "And what is your theory of me?"

"That you are very peculiar."

"How?"

"You are proud."

"And is pride so very peculiar?"

"Yes; in women."

"Indeed! You set up for a connoisseur of female character. That's very common, nowadays. Why don't you tell me something more about Yourself? We're always talking about me."

He might well have been doubtful of her humor. He seemed to decide that she was jesting, for he answered lightly, "Why, you began it."

"I know I did, this time. But now I wish to stop it, too."

He looked down at the tiller in his hands. "Well," he said, "I should like to tell you about myself. I should like to know what you think of the kind of man I am. Will you be honest if I will?"

"That's a very strange condition," she answered, meeting and then avoiding the gaze he lifted to her face.

"What? Being honest?"

"Well, no - Or, yes!"

"It isn't for you."

"Thank you. But I'm not under discussion now."

"Well, in the first place," he began, "I was afraid of you when we met."

"Afraid of me?"

"That isn't the word, perhaps. We'll say ashamed of myself. Mrs. Maynard told me about you, and I thought you would despise me for not doing or being anything in particular. I thought you must."

"Indeed!"

He hesitated, as if still uncertain of her mood from this intonation, and then he went on: "But I had some little hope you would tolerate me, after all. You looked like a friend I used to have. - Do you mind my telling you?"

"Oh, no. Though I can't say that it's ever very comfortable to be told that you look like some one else."

"I don't suppose any one else would have been struck by the resemblance," said Libby, with a laugh of reminiscence. "He was huge. But he had eyes like a girl, - I beg your pardon, - like yours."

"You mean that I have eyes like a man."

He laughed, and said, "No," and then turned grave. "As long as he lived" -

"Oh, is he dead?" she asked more gently than she had yet spoken.

"Yes, he died just before I went abroad. I went out on business for my father, - he's an importer and jobber, - and bought goods for him. Do you despise business?"

"I don't know anything about it."

"I did it to please my father, and he said I was a very good buyer. He thinks there's nothing like buying - except selling. He used to sell things himself, over the counter, and not so long ago, either.

"I fancied it made a difference for me when I was in college, and that the yardstick came between me and society. I was an ass for thinking anything about it. Though I didn't really care, much. I never liked society, and I did like boats and horses. I thought of a profession, once. But it wouldn't work. I've been round the world twice, and I've done nothing but enjoy myself since I left college, - or try to. When I first saw you I was hesitating about letting my father make me of use. He wants me to become one of the most respectable members of society, he wants me to be a cotton-spinner. You know there's nothing so irreproachable as cotton, for a business?"

"No. I don't know about those things."

"Well, there isn't. When I was abroad, buying and selling, I made a little discovery: I found that there were goods we could make and sell in the European market cheaper than the English, and that gave my father the notion of buying a mill to make them. I'm boring you!"

"No."

"Well, he bought it; and he wants me to take charge of it."

"And shall you?"

"Do you think I'm fit for it?"

"I? How should I know?"

"You don't know cotton; but you know me a little. Do I strike you as fit for anything?" She made no reply to this, and he laughed. "I assure you I felt small enough when I heard what you had done, and thought - what I had done. It gave me a start; and I wrote my father that night that I would go in for it."

"I once thought of going to a factory town," she answered, without wilful evasion, "to begin my practice there among the operatives' children. I should have done it if it had not been for coming here with Mrs. Maynard. It would have been better."

"Come to my factory town, Miss Breen! There ought to be

William Dean Howells

fevers there in the autumn, with all the low lands that I'm allowed to flood Mrs. Maynard told me about your plan."

"Pray, what else did Mrs. Maynard tell you about me?"

"About your taking up a profession, in the way you did, when you needn't, and when you didn't particularly like it."

"Oh!" she said. Then she added, "And because I wasn't obliged to it, and didn't like it, you tolerated me?"

"Tolerated?" he echoed.

This vexed her. "Yes, tolerate! Everybody, interested or not, has to make up his mind whether to tolerate me as soon as he hears what I am. What excuse did you make for me?"

"I didn't make any," said Libby.

"But you had your misgiving, your surprise."

"I thought if you could stand it, other people might. I thought it was your affair."

"Just as if I had been a young man?"

"No! That wasn't possible."

She was silent. Then, "The conversation has got back into the old quarter," she said. "You are talking about me again. Have you heard from your friends since they went away?"

"What friends?"

"Those you were camping with."

"No."

"What did they say when they heard that you had found a

young doctress at Jocelyn's? How did you break the fact to them? What jokes did they make? You needn't be afraid to tell me!" she cried. "Give me Mr. Johnson's comments."

He looked at her in surprise that incensed her still more, and rendered her incapable of regarding the pain with which he answered her. "I 'm afraid," he said, "that I have done something to offend you."

"Oh no! What could you have done?"

"Then you really mean to ask me whether I would let any one make a joke of you in my presence?"

"Yes; why not?"

"Because it was impossible," he answered.

"Why was it impossible?" she pursued.

"Because - I love you."

She had been looking him defiantly in the eyes, and she could not withdraw her gaze. For the endless moment that ensued, her breath was taken away. Then she asked in a low, steady voice, "Did you mean to say that?"

"No."

"I believe you, and I forgive you. No, no!" she cried, at a demonstration of protest from him, "don't speak again!"

He obeyed, instantly, implicitly. With the tiller in his hand he looked past her and guided the boat's course. It became intolerable.

"Have I ever done anything that gave you the right to - to - say that?" she asked, without the self-command which she might have wished to show.

"No," he said, "you were only the most beautiful" -

"I am not beautiful! And if I were" -

"It wasn't to be helped! I saw from the first how good and noble you were, and" -

"This is absurd!" she exclaimed. "I am neither good nor noble; and if I were" -

"It wouldn't make any difference. Whatever you are, you are the one woman in the world to me; and you always will be."

"Mr. Libby!"

"Oh, I must speak now! You were always thinking, because you had studied a man's profession, that no one would think of you as a woman, as if that could make any difference to a man that had the soul of a man in him!"

"No, no!" she protested. "I didn't think that. I always expected to be considered as a woman."

"But not as a woman to fall in love with. I understood. And that somehow made you all the dearer to me. If you had been a girl like other girls, I shouldn't have cared for you."

"Oh!"

"I didn't mean to speak to you to-day. But sometime I did mean to speak; because, whatever I was, I loved you; and I thought you didn't dislike me."

"I did like you," she murmured, "very much. And I respected you. But you can't say that I ever gave you any hope in this - this - way." She almost asked him if she had.

"No, - not purposely. And if you did, it's over now. You have rejected me. I understand that. There's no reason why you shouldn't. And I can hold my tongue." He did not turn, but looked steadily past her at the boat's head.

An emotion stirred in her breast which took the form of a reproach. "Was it fair, then, to say this when neither of us could escape afterwards?"

"I didn't mean to speak," he said, without looking up, "and I never meant to place you where you couldn't escape."

It was true that she had proposed to go with him in the boat, and that she had chosen to come back with him, when he had offered to have her driven home from Leyden. "No, you are not to blame," she said, at last. "I asked to some with you. Shall I tell you why?" Her voice began to break. In her pity for him and her shame for herself the tears started to her eyes. She did not press her question, but, "Thank you for reminding me that I invited myself to go with you," she said, with feeble bitterness.

He looked up at her in silent wonder, and she broke into a sob. He said gently, "I don't suppose you expect me to deny that. You don't think me such a poor dog as that."

"Why, of course not," she answered, with quivering lips, while she pressed her handkerchief to her eyes.

"I was only too glad to have you come. I always meant to tell you - what I have told; but not when I should seem to trap you into listening."

"No," she murmured, "I can believe that of you. I do believe it. I take back what I said. Don't let us speak of it any more now," she continued, struggling for her lost composure, with what success appeared in the fresh outburst with which she recognized his forbearance to hint at any painfulness to himself in the situation.

"I don't mind it so much on my account, but oh! how could

you for your own sake? Do let us get home as fast as we can!"

"I am doing everything I can to release you," he said. "If you will sit here," he added, indicating the place beside him in the stern, "you won't have to change so much when I want to tack."

She took the other seat, and for the first time she noticed that the wind had grown very light. She watched him with a piteous impatience while he shifted the sail from side to side, keeping the sheet in his hand for convenience in the frequent changes. He scanned the sky, and turned every current of the ebbing tide to account. It was useless; the boat crept, and presently it scarcely moved.

"The wind is down," he said, making the sheet fast, and relaxing his hold on the tiller.

"And - And the tide is going out!" she exclaimed.

"The tide is going out," he admitted.

"If we should get caught on these flats," she began, with rising indignation.

"We should have to stay till the tide turned."

She looked wildly about for aid. If there were a row-boat anywhere within hail, she could be taken to Jocelyn's in that. But they were quite alone on those lifeless waters.

Libby got out a pair of heavy oars from the bottom of the boat, and, setting the rowlocks on either side, tugged silently at them.

The futile effort suggested an idea to her which doubtless she would not have expressed if she had not been lacking, as she once said, in a sense of humor.

"Why don't you whistle for a wind?"

He stared at her in sad astonishment to make sure that she was in earnest, and then, "Whistle!" he echoed forlornly, and broke into a joyless laugh.

"You knew the chances of delay that I took in asking to come with you," she cried, "and you should have warned me. It was ungenerous - it was ungentlemanly!"

"It was whatever you like. I must be to blame. I suppose I was too glad to have you come. If I thought anything, I thought you must have some particular errand at Leyden. You seemed anxious to go, even if it stormed."

"If it had stormed," she retorted, "I should not have cared! I hoped it would storm. Then at least I should have run the same danger, - I hoped it would be dangerous."

"I don't understand what you mean," he said.

"I forced that wretched creature to go with you that day when you said it was going to be rough; and I shall have her blood upon my hands if she dies."

"Is it possible," cried Libby, pulling in his useless oars, and leaning forward upon them, "that she has gone on letting you think I believed there was going to be a storm? She knew perfectly well that I didn't mind what Adams said; he was always croaking." She sat looking at him in a daze, but she could not speak, and he continued. "I see: it happened by one chance in a million to turn out as he said; and she has been making you pay for it. Why, I suppose," he added, with a melancholy smile of intelligence, "she's had so much satisfaction in holding you responsible for what's happened, that she's almost glad of it!"

"She has tortured me!" cried the girl. "But you - you, when you saw that I didn't believe there was going to be any storm, why did you - why didn't - you" -

"I didn't believe it either! It was Mrs. Maynard that proposed the sail, but when I saw that you didn't like it I was glad of any excuse for putting it off. I couldn't help wanting to please you, and I couldn't see why you urged us afterwards; but I supposed you had some reason."

She passed her hand over her forehead, as if to clear away the confusion in which all this involved her. "But why - why did you let me go on thinking myself to blame" -

"How could I know what you were thinking? Heaven knows I didn't dream of such a thing! Though I remember, now, your saying" -

"Oh, I see!" she cried. "You are a man! But I can't forgive it, - no, I can't forgive it! You wished to deceive her if you didn't wish to deceive me. How can you excuse yourself for repeating what you didn't believe?"

"I was willing she should think Adams was right."

"And that was deceit. What can you say to it?"

"There is only one thing I could say," he murmured, looking hopelessly into her eyes, "and that's of no use."

She turned her head away. Her tragedy had fallen to nothing; or rather it had never been. All her remorse, all her suffering, was mere farce now; but his guilt in the matter was the greater. A fierce resentment burned in her heart; she longed to make him feel something of the anguish she had needlessly undergone.

He sat watching her averted face. "Miss Breen," he said huskily, "will you let me speak to you?"

"Oh, you have me in your power," she answered cruelly. "Say

what you like."

He did not speak, nor make any motion to do so.

A foolish, idle curiosity to know what, after all that had happened, he could possibly have to say, stirred within her, but she disdainfully stifled it. They were both so still that a company of seals found it safe to put their heads above water, and approach near enough to examine her with their round soft eyes. She turned from the silly things in contempt that they should even have interested her. She felt that from time to time her companion lifted an anxious glance to the dull heavens. At last the limp sail faintly stirred; it flapped; it filled shallowly; the boat moved. The sail seemed to have had a prescience of the wind before it passed over the smooth water like a shadow.

When a woman says she never will forgive a man, she always has a condition of forgiveness in her heart. Now that the wind had risen again, "I have no right to forbid you to speak," she said, as if no silence had elapsed, and she turned round and quietly confronted him; she no longer felt so impatient to escape.

He did not meet her eye at once, and he seemed in no haste to avail himself of the leave granted him. A heavy sadness blotted the gayety of a face whose sunny sympathy had been her only cheer for many days. She fancied a bewilderment in its hopelessness which smote her with still sharper pathos. "Of course," she said, "I appreciate your wish to do what I wanted, about Mrs. Maynard. I remember my telling you that she oughtn't to go out, that day. But that was not the way to do it" -

"There was no other," he said.

"No," she assented, upon reflection. "Then it oughtn't to have been done."

He showed no sign of intending to continue, and after a moment of restlessness, she began again.

"If I have been rude or hasty in refusing to hear you, Mr. Libby, I am very wrong. I must hear anything you have to say."

"Oh, not unless you wish."

"I wish whatever you wish."

"I'm not sure that I wish that now. I have thought it over; I should only distress you for nothing. You are letting me say why sentence shouldn't be passed upon me. Sentence is going to be passed any way. I should only repeat what I have said. You would pity me, but you couldn't help me. And that would give you pain for nothing. No, it would be useless."

"It would be useless to talk to me about - loving." She took the word on her lips with a certain effect of adopting it for convenience' sake in her vocabulary. "All that was ended for me long ago, - ten years ago. And my whole life since then has been shaped to do without it. I will tell you my story if you like. Perhaps it's your due. I wish to be just. You may have a right to know."

"No, I haven't. But - perhaps I ought to say that Mrs. Maynard told me something."

"Well, I am glad of that, though she had no right to do it. Then you can understand."

"Oh, yes, I can understand. I don't pretend that I had any reason in it."

He forbore again to urge any plea for himself, and once more she was obliged to interfere in his behalf. "Mr. Libby, I have never confessed that I once wronged you in a way that I'm very sorry for."

"About Mrs. Maynard? Yes, I know. I won't try to whitewash myself; but it didn't occur to me how it would look. I wanted to talk with her about you."

"You ought to have considered her, though," she said gently.

"She ought to have considered herself," he retorted, with his unfailing bitterness for Mrs. Maynard. "But it doesn't matter whose fault it was. I'm sufficiently punished; for I know that it injured me with you."

"It did at first. But now I can see that I was wrong. I wished to tell you that. It isn't creditable to me that I thought you intended to flirt with her. If I had been better myself' -

"You!" He could not say more.

That utter faith in her was very charming. It softened her more and more; it made her wish to reason with him, and try gently to show him how impossible his hope was. "And you know," she said, recurring to something that had gone before, "that even if I had cared for you in the way you wish, it couldn't be. You wouldn't want to have people laughing and saying I had been a doctress."

"I shouldn't have minded. I know how much people's talk is worth."

"Yes," she said, "I know you would be generous and brave about that - about anything. But what - what if I couldn't give up my career - my hopes of being useful in the way I have planned? You wouldn't have liked me to go on practising medicine?"

"I thought of that," he answered simply. "I didn't see how it could be done. But if you saw any way, I was willing - No, that was my great trouble! I knew that it was selfish in me, and very conceited, to suppose you would give up your whole life for me; and whenever I thought of that, I determined not to ask

William Dean Howells

you. But I tried not to think of that."

"Well, don't you see? But if I could have answered you as you wish, it wouldn't have been anything to give up everything for you. A woman isn't something else first, and a woman afterwards. I understand how unselfishly you meant, and indeed, indeed, I thank you. But don't let's talk of it any more. It couldn't have been, and there is nothing but misery in thinking of it. Come," she said, with a struggle for cheerfulness, "let us forget it. Let it be just as if you hadn't spoken to me; I know you didn't intend to do it; and let us go on as if nothing had happened."

"Oh, we can't go on," he answered. "I shall get away, as soon as Maynard comes, and rid you of the sight of me."

"Are you going away?" she softly asked. "Why need you? I know that people always seem to think they can't be friends after - such a thing as this. But why shouldn't we? I respect you, and I like you very much. You have shown me more regard and more kindness than any other friend" -

"But I wasn't your friend," he interrupted. "I loved you."

"Well," she sighed, in gentle perplexity, "then you can't be my friend?"

"Never. But I shall always love you. If it would do any good, I would stay, as you ask it. I shouldn't mind myself. But I should be a nuisance to you."

"No, no!" she exclaimed. "I will take the risk of that. I need your advice, your - sympathy, your - You won't trouble me, indeed you won't. Perhaps you have mistaken your - feeling about me. It's such a very little time since we met," she pleaded.

"That makes no difference, - the time. And I'm not mistaken."

"Well, stay at least till Mrs. Maynard is well, and we can all go away together. Promise me that!" She instinctively put out her hand toward him in entreaty. He took it, and pressing it to his lips covered it with kisses.

"Oh!" she grieved in reproachful surprise.

"There!" he cried. "You see that I must go!"

"Yes," she sighed in assent, "you must go."

They did not look at each other again, but remained in a lamentable silence while the boat pushed swiftly before the freshening breeze; and when they reached the place where the dory lay, he dropped the sail and threw out the anchor without a word.

He was haggard to the glance she stole at him, when they had taken their places in the dory, and he confronted her, pulling hard at the oars. He did not lift his eyes to hers, but from time to time he looked over his shoulder at the boat's prow, and he rowed from one point to another for a good landing. A dreamy pity for him filled her; through the memories of her own suffering, she divined the soreness of his heart.

She started from her reverie as the bottom of the dory struck the sand. The shoal water stretched twenty feet beyond. He pulled in the oars and rose desperately. "It's of no use: I shall have to carry you ashore."

She sat staring up into his face, and longing to ask him something, to accuse him of having done this purposely. But she had erred in so many doubts, her suspicions of him had all recoiled so pitilessly upon her, that she had no longer the courage to question or reproach him. "Oh, no, thank you," she said weakly. "I won't trouble you. I - I will wait till the tide is out."

"The tide's out now," he answered with coldness, "and you

William Dean Howells

can't wade."

She rose desperately. "Why, of course!" she cried in self-contempt, glancing at the water, into which he promptly stepped to his boot-tops. "A woman mustn't get her feet wet."

VIII

Grace went to her own room to lay aside her shawl and hat, before going to Mrs. Maynard, and found her mother sewing there.

"Why, who is with Mrs. Maynard?" she asked.

"Miss Gleason is reading to her," said Mrs. Breen. "If she had any sort of active treatment, she could get well at once. I couldn't take the responsibility of doing anything for her, and it was such a worry to stay and see everything going wrong, that when Miss Gleason came in I was glad to get away. Miss Gleason seems to believe in your Dr. Mulbridge."

"My Dr. Mulbridge!" echoed Grace.

"She talked of him as if he were yours. I don't know what you've been saying to her about him; but you had better be careful. The woman is a fool." She now looked up at her daughter for the first time. "Why, what is the matter with you what kept you so long? You look perfectly wild."

"I feel wild," said Grace calmly. "The wind went down."

"Was that all? I don't see why that should make you feel wild," said her mother, dropping her spectacles to her sewing again.

"It wasn't all," answered the girl, sinking provisionally upon the side of a chair, with her shawl still on her arm, and her hat

William Dean Howells

in her hand. "Mother, have you noticed anything peculiar about Mr. Libby?"

"He's the only person who seems to be of the slightest use about here; I've noticed that," said Mrs. Breen. "He's always going and coming for you and Mrs. Maynard. Where is that worthless husband of hers? Hasn't he had time to come from Cheyenne yet?"

"He's on the way. He was out at his ranch when Mr. Libby telegraphed first, and had to be sent for. We found a despatch from him at Leyden, saying he had started," Grace explained.

"What business had he to be so far away at all?" demanded her mother. It was plain that Mrs. Breen was in her most censorious temper, which had probably acquired a sharper edge towards Maynard from her reconciliation with his wife.

Grace seized her chance to meet the worst. "Do you think that I have done anything to encourage Mr. Libby?" she asked, looking bravely at her mother.

"Encourage him to do what?" asked Mrs. Breen, without lifting her eyes from her work.

"Encouraged him to - think I cared for him; to - to be in love with me."

Mrs. Breen lifted her head now, and pushed her spectacles up on her forehead, while she regarded her daughter in silence. "Has he been making love to you?"

"Yes."

Her mother pushed her spectacles down again; and, turning the seam which she had been sewing, flattened it with her thumb-nail. She made this action expressive of having foreseen such a result, and of having struggled against it, neglected and alone. "Very well, then. I hope you accepted him?" she asked quietly.

"Mother!"

"Why not? You must like him," she continued in the same tone. "You have been with him every moment the last week that you haven't been with Mrs. Maynard. At least I've seen nothing of you, except when you came to tell me you were going to walk or to drive with him. You seem to have asked him to take you most of the time."

"How can you say such a thing, mother?" cried the girl.

"Didn't you ask him to let you go with him this afternoon? You told me you did."

"Yes, I did. I did it for a purpose."

"Ah! for a purpose," said Mrs. Breen, taking a survey of the new seam, which she pulled from her knee, where one end of it was pinned, towards her chin. She left the word to her daughter, who was obliged to take it.

"I asked him to let me go with him because Louise had tortured me about making her go out in his boat, till I couldn't bear it any longer. It seemed to me that if I took the same risk myself, it would be something; and I hoped there would be a storm."

"I should think you had taken leave of your senses," Mrs. Breen observed, with her spectacles intent upon her seam. "Did you think it would be any consolation to him if you were drowned, or to her? And if," she added, her conscience rising equal to the vicarious demand upon it, "you hoped there would be danger, had you any right to expose him to it? Even if you chose to risk your own life, you had no right to risk his." She lifted her spectacles again, and turned their austere glitter upon her daughter.

William Dean Howells

"Yes, it all seems very silly now," said the girl, with a hopeless sigh.

"Silly!" cried her mother. "I'm glad you can call it silly."

"And it seemed worse still when he told me that he had never believed it was going to storm that day, when he took Louise out. His man said it was, and he repeated it because he saw I didn't want her to go."

"Perhaps," suggested Mrs. Breen, "if he was willing to deceive her then, he is willing to deceive you now."

"He didn't deceive her. He said what he had heard. And he said it because he - I wished it."

"I call it deceiving. Truth is truth. That is what I was taught; and that's what I supposed I had taught you."

"I would trust Mr. Libby in anything," returned the daughter. "He is perfectly frank about himself. He confessed that he had done it to please me. He said that nothing else could excuse it."

"Oh, then you have accepted him!"

"No, mother, I haven't. I have refused him, and he is going away as soon as Mr. Maynard comes." She sat looking at the window, and the tears stole into her eyes, and blurred the sea and sky together where she saw their meeting at the horizon line.

"Well," said her mother, "their that is the end of it, I presume."

"Yes, that's the end," said Grace. "But - I felt sorry for him, mother. Once," she went on, "I thought I had everything clear before me; but now I seem only to have made confusion of my life. Yes," she added drearily, "it was foolish and wicked, and it was perfectly useless, too. I can't escape from the consequences of what I did. It makes no difference what he believed or any one believed. I drove them on to risk their lives because I thought myself so much better than they; because I was self-righteous and suspicious and stubborn. Well, I must bear the penalty: and oh, if I could only bear it alone!" With a long sigh she took back the burden which she had been struggling to cast off, and from which for a time she had actually seemed to escape. She put away her hat and shawl, and stood before the glass, smoothing her hair. "When will it ever end?" she moaned to the reflection there, rather than to her mother, who did not interrupt this spiritual ordeal. In another age, such a New England girl would have tortured herself with inquisition as to some neglected duty to God; - in ours, when religion is so largely humanified, this Puritan soul could only wreak itself in a sense of irreparable wrong to her fellow-creature.

When she went out she met Miss Gleason half-way down the corridor to Mrs. Maynard's door. The latter had a book in her hand, and came forward whispering. "She's asleep," she said very sibilantly. "I have read her to sleep, and she's sleeping beautifully. Have you ever read it?" she asked, with hoarse breaks from her undertone, as she held up one of those cheap library-editions of a novel toward Grace.

"Jane Eyre? Why, of course. Long ago."

"So have I," said Miss Gleason. "But I sent and got it again, to refresh my impressions of Rochester. We all think Dr. Mulbridge is just like him. Rochester is my ideal character, - a perfect conception of a man: so abrupt, so rough, so savage. Oh, I like those men! Don't you?" she fluted. "Mrs. Maynard sees the resemblance, as well as the rest of us. But I know! You don't approve of them. I suppose they can't be defended on some grounds; but I can see how, even in such a case as this, the perfect mastery of the man-physician constitutes the highest usefulness of the woman-physician. The advancement of women must be as women. 'Male and female created he them,' and it is only in remembering this that we are helping

William Dean Howells

Gawd, whether as an anthropomorphic conception or a universally pervading instinct of love, don't you think?"

With her novel clapped against her breast, she leaned winningly over toward Grace, and fixed her with her wide eyes, which had rings of white round the pupils.

"Do tell me!" she ran on without waiting an answer. "Didn't you go with Mr. Libby because you hoped it might storm, and wished to take the same risk as Mrs. Maynard? I told Mrs. Alger you did!"

Grace flushed guiltily, and Miss Gleason cowered a little, perhaps interpreting the color as resentment. "I should consider that a very silly motive," she said, helplessly ashamed that she was leaving the weight of the blow upon Miss Gleason's shoulders instead of her own.

"Of course," said Miss Gleason enthusiastically, "you can't confess it. But I know you are capable of such a thing - of anything heroic! Do forgive me," she said, seizing Grace's hand. She held it a moment, gazing with a devouring fondness into her face, which she stooped a little sidewise to peer up into. Then she quickly dropped her hand, and, whirling away, glided slimly out of the corridor.

Grace softly opened Mrs. Maynard's door, and the sick woman opened her eyes. "I wasn't asleep," she said hoarsely, "but I had to pretend to be, or that woman would have killed me."

Grace went to her and felt her hands and her flushed forehead.

"I am worse this evening," said Mrs. Maynard.

"Oh, no," sighed the girl, dropping into a chair at the bedside, with her eyes fixed in a sort of fascination on the lurid face of the sick woman.

"After getting me here," continued Mrs. Maynard, in the same low, hoarse murmur, "you might at least stay with me a little. What kept you so long?"

"The wind fell. We were becalmed."

"We were not becalmed the day I went out with Mr. Libby. But perhaps nobody forced you to go."

Having launched this dart, she closed her eyes again with something more like content than she had yet shown: it had an aim of which she could always be sure.

"We have heard from Mr. Maynard," said Grace humbly. "There was a despatch waiting for Mr. Libby at Leyden. He is on his way."

Mrs. Maynard betrayed no immediate effect of this other than to say, "He had better hurry," and did not open her eyes.

Grace went about the room with a leaden weight in every fibre, putting the place in order, and Mrs. Maynard did not speak again till she had finished. Then she said, "I want you to tell me just how bad Dr. Mulbridge thinks I am."

"He has never expressed any anxiety," Grace began, with her inaptness at evasion.

"Of course he hasn't," murmured the sick woman. "He isn't a fool! What does he say?"

This passed the sufferance even of remorse. "He says you mustn't talk," the girl flashed out. "And if you insist upon doing so, I will leave you, and send some one else to take care of you."

"Very well, then. I know what that means. When a doctor tells you not to talk, it's because he knows he can't do you any good. As soon as George Maynard gets here I will have some one that can cure me, or I will know the reason why." The conception of her husband as a champion seemed to commend him to her in novel degree. She shed some tears, and after a little reflection she asked, "How soon will he be here?"

"I don't know," said Grace. "He seems to have started yesterday morning."

"He can be here by day after to-morrow," Mrs. Maynard computed. "There will be some one to look after poor little Bella then," she added, as if, during her sickness, Bella must have been wholly neglected. "Don't let the child be all dirt when her father comes."

"Mother will look after Bella," Grace replied, too meek again to resent the implication. After a pause, "Oh, Louise," she added beseechingly, "I've suffered so much from my own wrong-headedness and obstinacy that I couldn't bear to see you taking the same risk, and I'm so glad that you are going to meet your husband in the right spirit."

"What right spirit?" croaked Mrs. Maynard.

"The wish to please him, to" -

"I don't choose to have him say that his child disgraces him," replied Mrs. Maynard, in the low, husky, monotonous murmur in which she was obliged to utter everything.

"But, dear Louise!" cried the other, "you choose something else too, don't you? You wish to meet him as if no unkindness had parted you, and as if you were to be always together after this? I hope you do! Then I should feel that all this suffering and, trouble was a mercy."

"Other people's misery is always a mercy to them," hoarsely suggested Mrs. Maynard.

"Yes, I know that," Grace submitted, with meek conviction. "But, Louise," she pleaded, "you will make up with your husband, won't you? Whatever he has done, that will surely be best. I know that you love him, and that he must love you, yet. It's the only way. If you were finally separated from him, and you and he could be happy apart, what would become of that poor child? Who will take a father's place with her? That's the worst about it. Oh, Louise, I feel so badly for you - for what you have lost, and may lose. Marriage must change people so that unless they live to each other, their lives will be maimed and useless. It ought to be so much easier to forgive any wrong your husband does you than to punish it; for that perpetuates the wrong, and forgiveness ends it, and it's the only thing that can end a wrong. I am sure that your husband will be ready to do or say anything you wish; but if he shouldn't, Louise, you will receive him forgivingly, and make the first advance? It's a woman's right to make the advances in forgiving."

Mrs. Maynard lay with her hands stretched at her side under the covering, and only her face visible above it. She now turned her head a little, so as to pierce the earnest speaker with a gleam from her dull eye. "Have you accepted Walter Libby?" she asked.

"Louise!" cried Grace, with a blush that burned like fire.

"That's the way I used to talk when I was first engaged. Wait till you're married a while. I want Bella to have on her pique, and her pink sash, - not the cherry one. I should think you would have studied to be a minister instead of a doctor. But you needn't preach to me; I shall know how to behave to George Maynard when he comes, - if he ever does come. And now I should think you had made me talk enough!"

"Yes, Yes," said Grace, recalled to her more immediate duty in alarm.

All her helpfulness was soon to be needed. The disease, which had lingered more than usual in the early stages, suddenly approached a crisis. That night Mrs. Maynard grew so much worse that Grace sent Libby at daybreak for Dr. Mulbridge;

and the young man, after leading out his own mare to see if her lameness had abated, ruefully put her back in the stable, and set off to Corbitant with the splay-foot at a rate of speed unparalleled, probably, in the animal's recollection of a long and useful life. In the two anxious days that followed, Libby and Grace were associated in the freedom of a common interest outside of themselves; she went to him for help and suggestion, and he gave them, as if nothing had passed to restrict or embarrass their relations. There was that, in fact, in the awe of the time and an involuntary disoccupation of hers that threw them together even more constantly than before. Dr. Mulbridge remained with his patient well into the forenoon; in the afternoon he came again, and that night he did not go away. He superseded Grace as a nurse no less completely than he had displaced her as a physician. He let her relieve him when he flung himself down for a few minutes' sleep, or when he went out for the huge meals which he devoured, preferring the unwholesome things with a depravity shocking to the tender physical consciences of the ladies who looked on; but when he returned to his charge, he showed himself jealous of all that Grace had done involving the exercise of more than a servile discretion. When she asked him once if there were nothing else that she could do, he said, "fires, keep those women and children quiet," in a tone that classed her with both. She longed to ask him what he thought of Mrs. May nard's condition; but she had not the courage to invoke the intelligence that ignored her so completely, and she struggled in silence with such disheartening auguries as her theoretical science enabled her to make.

The next day was a Sunday, and the Sabbath hush which always hung over Jocelyn's was intensified to the sense of those who ached between hope and fear for the life that seemed to waver and flicker in that still air. Dr. Mulbridge watched beside his patient, noting every change with a wary intelligence which no fact escaped and no anxiety clouded; alert, gentle, prompt; suffering no question, and absolutely silent as to all impressions. He allowed Grace to remain with him when she liked, and let her do his bidding in minor matters; but when from time to time she escaped from the intolerable tension in which his reticence and her own fear held her, he did not seem to see whether she went or came. Toward nightfall she met him coming out of Mrs. Maynard's room, as she drew near in the narrow corridor.

"Where is your friend - the young man - the one who smokes?" he asked, as if nothing unusual had occupied him. "I want him to give me a cigar."

"Dr. Mulbridge," she said, "I will not bear this any longer. I must know the worst - you have no right to treat me in this way. Tell me now - tell me instantly: will she live?"

He looked at her with an imaginable apprehension of hysterics, but as she continued firm, and placed herself resolutely in his way, he relaxed his scrutiny, and said, with a smile, "Oh, I think so. What made you think she wouldn't?"

She drew herself aside, and made way far him.

"Go!" she cried. She would have said more, but her indignation choked her.

He did not pass at once, and he did not seem troubled at her anger. "Dr. Breen," he said, "I saw a good deal of pneumonia in the army, and I don't remember a single case that was saved by the anxiety of the surgeon."

He went now, as people do when they fancy themselves to have made a good point; and she heard him asking Barlow for Libby, outside, and then walking over the gravel toward the stable. At that moment she doubted and hated him so much that she world have been glad to keep Libby from talking or even smoking with him. But she relented a little toward him afterwards, when he returned and resumed the charge of his patient with the gentle, vigilant cheerfulness which she had admired in him from the first, omitting no care and betraying none. He appeared to take it for granted that Grace saw an

William Dean Howells

improvement, but he recognized it by nothing explicit till he rose and said, "I think I will leave Mrs. Maynard with you to-night, Dr. Breen."

The sick woman's eyes turned to him imploringly from her pillow, and Grace spoke the terror of both when she faltered in return, "Are you - you are not going home?"

"I shall sleep in the house."

"Oh, thank you!" she cried fervently.

"And you can call me if you wish. But there won't be any occasion. Mrs. Maynard is very much better." He waited to give, in a sort of absent-minded way, certain directions. Then he went out, and Grace sank back into the chair from which she had started at his rising, and wept long and silently with a hidden face. When she took away her hands and dried her tears, she saw Mrs. Maynard beckoning to her. She went to the bedside.

"What is it, dear?" she asked tenderly.

"Stoop down," whispered the other; and as Grace bowed her ear Mrs. Maynard touched her cheek with her dry lips. In this kiss doubtless she forgave the wrong which she had hoarded in her heart, and there perverted into a deadly injury. But they both knew upon what terms the pardon was accorded, and that if Mrs. Maynard had died, she would have died holding Grace answerable for her undoing.

IX

In the morning Dr. Mulbridge drove back to Corbitant, and in the evening Libby came over from New Leyden with Maynard, in a hired wagon. He was a day later than his wife had computed, but as she appeared to have reflected, she had left the intervening Sunday out of her calculation; this was one of the few things she taxed herself to say. For the rest, she seemed to be hoarding her strength against his coming.

Grace met him at a little distance from the house, whither she had walked with Bella, for a breath of the fresh air after her long day in the sick-room, and did not find him the boisterous and jovial Hoosier she had imagined him. It was, in fact, hardly the moment for the expression of Western humor. He arrived a sleep-broken, travel-creased figure, with more than the Western man's usual indifference to dress; with sad, dull eyes, and an untrimmed beard that hung in points and tags, and thinly hid the corners of a large mouth. He took her hand laxly in his, and bowing over her from his lank height listened to her report of his wife's state, while he held his little girl on his left arm, and the child fondly pressed her cheek against his bearded face, to which he had quietly lifted her as soon as he alighted from Libby's buggy.

Libby introduced Grace as Dr. Breen, and drove on, and Maynard gave her the title whenever he addressed her, with a perfect effect of single-mindedness in his gravity, as if it were an every-day thing with him to meet young ladies who were physicians. He had a certain neighborly manner of having

William Dean Howells

known her a long time, and of being on good terms with her; and somewhere there resided in his loosely knit organism a powerful energy. She had almost to run in keeping at his side, as he walked on to the house, carrying his little girl on his arm, and glancing about him; and she was not sure at last that she had succeeded in making him understand how serious the case had been.

"I don't know whether I ought to let you go in," she said, "without preparing her."

"She's been expecting me, hasn't she?" he asked.

"Yes, but" -

"And she's awake?"

"Then I'll just go in and prepare her myself. I'm a pretty good hand at preparing people to meet me. You've a beautiful location here, Dr. Breen; and your town has a chance to grow. I like to see a town have some chance," he added, with a sadness past tears in his melancholy eyes. "Bella can show me the way to the room, I reckon," he said, setting the little one down on the piazza, and following her indoors; and when Grace ventured, later, to knock at the door, Maynard's voice bade her come in.

He sat beside his wife's pillow, with her hand in his left; on his right arm perched the little girl, and rested her head on his shoulder. They did not seem to have been talking, and they did not move when Grace entered the room. But, apparently, Mrs. Maynard had known how to behave to George Maynard, and peace was visibly between them.

"Now, you tell me about the medicines, Dr. Breen, and then you go and get some rest," said Maynard in his mild, soothing voice. "I used to understand Mrs. Maynard's ways pretty well, and I can take care of her. Libby told me all about you and your doings, and I know you must feel as pale as you look."

"But you can't have had any sleep on the way," Grace began.

"Sleep?" Maynard repeated, looking wanly at her. "I never sleep. I'd as soon think of digesting."

After she had given him the needed instructions he rose from the rocking-chair in-which he had been softly swinging to and fro, and followed her out into the corridor, caressing with his large hand the child that lay on his shoulder. "Of course," she said, "Mrs. Maynard is still very sick, and needs the greatest care and attention."

"Yes, I understand that. But I reckon it will come out all right in the end," he said, with the optimistic fatalism which is the real religion of our orientalizing West. "Good-night, doctor."

She went away, feeling suddenly alone in this exclusion from the cares that had absorbed her. There was no one on the piazza, which the moonlight printed with the shadows of the posts and the fanciful jigsaw work of the arches between them. She heard a step on the sandy walk round the corner, and waited wistfully.

It was Barlow who came in sight, as she knew at once, but she asked, "Mr. Barlow?"

"Yes'm," said Barlow. "What can I do for you?"

"Nothing. I thought it might be Mr. Libby at first. Do you know where he is?"

"Well, I know where he ain't," said Barlow; and having ineffectually waited to be questioned further, he added, "He ain't here, for one place. He's gone back to Leyden. He had to take that horse back."

"Oh!" she said.

"N' I guess he's goin' to stay."

"To stay? Where?"

"Well, there you've got me again. All I know is I've got to drive that mare of his'n over to-morrow, if I can git off, and next day if I can't. Didn't you know he was goin'?" asked Barlow, willing to recompense himself for the information he had given.

"Well!" he added sympathetically, at a little hesitation of hers:

Then she said, "I knew he must go. Good-night, Mr. Barlow," and went indoors. She remembered that he had said he would go as soon as Maynard came, and that she had consented that this would be best. But his going now seemed abrupt, though she approved it. She thought that she had something more to say to him, which might console him or reconcile him; she could not think what this was, but it left an indefinite longing, an unsatisfied purpose in her heart; and there was somewhere a tremulous sense of support withdrawn. Perhaps this was a mechanical effect of the cessation of her anxiety for Mrs. Maynard, which had been a support as well as a burden. The house was strangely quiet, as if some great noise had just been hushed, and it seemed empty. She felt timid in her room, but she dreaded the next day more than the dark. Her life was changed, and the future, which she had once planned so clearly, and had felt so strong to encounter, had fallen to a ruin, in which she vainly endeavored to find some clew or motive of the past. She felt remanded to the conditions of the girlhood that she fancied she had altogether outlived; she turned her face upon her pillow in a grief of bewildered aspiration and broken pride, and shed tears scarcely predicable of a doctor of medicine.

But there is no lapse or aberration of character which can be half so surprising to others as it is to one's self. She had resented Libby's treating her upon a theory, but she treated herself upon a theory, and we all treat ourselves upon a theory. We proceed each of us upon the theory that he is very brave, or generous, or gentle, or liberal, or truthful, or loyal, or just.

We may have the defects of our virtues, but nothing is more certain than that we have our virtues, till there comes a fatal juncture, not at all like the juncture in which we had often imagined ourselves triumphing against temptation. It passes, and the hero finds, to his dismay and horror, that he has run away; the generous man has been niggard; the gentleman has behaved like a ruffian, and the liberal like a bigot; the champion of truth has foolishly and vainly lied; the steadfast friend has betrayed his neighbor, the just person has oppressed him. This is the fruitful moment, apparently so sterile, in which character may spring and flower anew; but the mood of abject humility in which the theorist of his own character is plunged and struggles for his lost self-respect is full of deceit for others. It cannot last: it may end in disowning and retrieving the error, or it may end in justifying it, and building it into the reconstructed character, as something upon the whole unexpectedly fine; but it must end, for after all it is only a mood. In such a mood, in the anguish of her disappointment at herself, a woman clings to whatever support offers, and it is at his own risk that the man who chances to be this support accepts the weight with which she casts herself upon him as the measure of her dependence, though he may make himself necessary to her, if he has the grace or strength to do it.

Without being able to understand fully the causes of the dejection in which this girl seemed to appeal to him, Mulbridge might well have believed himself the man to turn it in his favor. If he did not sympathize with her distress, or even clearly divine it, still his bold generalizations, he found, always had their effect with women, whose natures are often to themselves such unknown territory that a man who assumes to know them has gone far to master them. He saw that a rude moral force alone seemed to have a charm with his lady patients, - women who had been bred to ease and wealth, and who had cultivated, if not very disciplined, minds. Their intellectual dissipation had apparently made them a different race from the simpler-hearted womenkind of his neighbors, apt to judge men in a sharp ignorance of what is fascinating in heroes; and it would not be strange if he included Grace in the

William Dean Howells

sort of contemptuous amusement with which he regarded these flatteringly dependent and submissive invalids. He at least did not conceive of her as she conceived of herself; but this may be impossible to any man with regard to any woman.

With his experience of other women's explicit and even eager obedience, the resistance which he had at first encountered in Grace gave zest to her final submission. Since he had demolished the position she had attempted to hold against him, he liked her for having imagined she could hold it; and she had continued to pique and interest him. He relished all her scruples and misgivings, and the remorse she had tried to confide to him; and if his enjoyment of these foibles of hers took too little account of her pain, it was never his characteristic to be tender of people in good health. He was, indeed, as alien to her Puritan spirit as if he had been born in Naples instead of Corbitant. He came of one of those families which one finds in nearly every New England community, as thoroughly New England in race as the rest, but flourishing in a hardy scepticism and contempt of the general sense. Whatever relation such people held to the old Puritan commonwealth when Puritanism was absolute, they must later have taken an active part in its disintegration, and were probably always a destructive force at its heart.

Mulbridge's grandfather was one of the last captains who sailed a slaver from Corbitant. When this commerce became precarious, he retired from the seas, took a young wife in second marriage, and passed his declining days in robust inebriety. He lived to cast a dying vote for General Jackson, and his son, the first Dr. Mulbridge, survived to illustrate the magnanimity of his fellow-townsmen during the first year of the civil war, as a tolerated Copperhead. Then he died, and his son, who was in the West, looking up a location for practice, was known to have gone out as surgeon with one of the regiments there. It was not supposed that he went from patriotism; but when he came back, a year before the end of the struggle, and settled in his native place, his service in the army was accepted among his old neighbors as evidence of a better disposition of some sort than had hitherto been attributable to any of his name.

In fact, the lazy, good-natured boy, whom they chiefly remembered before his college days, had always been well enough liked among those who had since grown to be first mates and ship captains in the little port where he was born and grew up. They had now all retired from the sea, and, having survived its manifold perils, were patiently waiting to be drowned in sail-boats on the bay. They were of the second generation of ships' captains still living in Corbitant; but they would be the last. The commerce of the little port had changed into the whaling trade in their time; this had ceased in turn, and the wharves had rotted away. Dr. Mulbridge found little practice among them; while attending their appointed fate, they were so thoroughly salted against decay as to preserve even their families. But he gradually gathered into his hands, from the clairvoyant and the Indian doctor, the business which they had shared between them since his father's death. There was here and there a tragical case of consumption among the farming families along the coast, and now and then a frightful accident among the fishermen; the spring and autumn brought their typhoid; the city people who came down to the neighboring hotels were mostly sick, or fell sick; and with the small property his father had left, he and his mother contrived to live.

They dwelt very harmoniously together; for his mother, who had passed more than a quarter of a century in strong resistance to her husband's will, had succumbed, as not uncommonly happens with such women, to the authority of her son, whom she had no particular pleasure or advantage in thwarting. In the phrase and belief of his neighbors, he took after her, rather than his father; but there was something ironical and baffling in him, which the local experts could not trace to either the Mulbridges or the Gardiners. They had a quiet, indifferent faith in his ability to make himself a position and name anywhere; but they were not surprised that he had come back to live in Corbitant, which was so manifestly the best place in the world, and which, if somewhat lacking in opportunity, was ample in the leisure they believed more congenial to him than success. Some of his lady patients at the hotels, who felt at times that they could not live without him, would have carried him back to the city with them by a gentle violence; but there was nothing in anything he said or did that betrayed ambition on his part. He liked to hear them talk, especially of their ideas of progress, as they called them, at which, with the ready adaptability of their sex, they joined him in laughing when they found that he could not take them seriously. The social, the emotional expression of the new scientific civilization struck him as droll, particularly in respect to the emancipation of women; and he sometimes gave these ladies the impression that he did not value woman's intellect at its true worth. He was far from light treatment of them, he was considerate of the distances that should be guarded; but he conveyed the sense of his scepticism as to their fitness for some things to which the boldest of them aspired.

His mother would have been willing to have him go to the city if he wished, but she was too ignorant of the world outside of Corbitant to guess at his possibilities in it, and such people as she had seen from it had not pleased her with it. Those summer-boarding lady patients who came to see him were sometimes suffered to wait with her till he came in, and they used to tell her how happy she must be to keep such a son with her, and twittered their patronage of her and her nice old-fashioned parlor, and their praises of his skill in such wise against her echoless silence that she conceived a strong repugnance for all their tribe, in which she naturally included Grace when she appeared. She had decided the girl to be particularly forth-putting, from something prompt and self-reliant in her manner that day; and she viewed with tacit disgust her son's toleration of a handsome young woman who had taken up a man's profession. They were not people who gossiped together, or confided in each other, and she would have known nothing and asked nothing from him about her, further than she had seen for herself. But Barlow had folks, as he called them, at Corbitant; and without her own connivance she had heard from them of all that was passing at Jocelyn's.

It was her fashion to approach any subject upon which she wished her son to talk as if they had already talked of it, and he accepted this convention with a perfect understanding that she thus expressed at once her deference to him and her resolution to speak whether he liked it or not. She had not asked him about Mrs. Maynard's sickness, or shown any interest in it; but after she learned from the Barlows that she was no longer in danger, she said to her son one morning, before he drove away upon his daily visit, "Is her husband going to stay with her, or is he going back?"

"I don't know, really," he answered, glancing at her where she sat erect across the table from him, with her hand on the lid of the coffee-pot, and her eyes downcast; it was the face of silent determination not to be put off, which he knew. "I don't suppose you care, mother," he added pleasantly.

"She's nothing to me," she assented. "What's that friend of hers going to do?"

"Which friend?"

"You know. The one that came after you."

"Oh! Dr. Breen. Yes. What did you think of her?"

"I don't see why you call her doctor."

"Oh, I do it out of politeness. Besides, she is one sort of doctor. Little pills," he added, with an enjoyment of his mother's grimness on this point.

"I should like to see a daughter of mine pretending to be a doctor," said Mrs. Mulbridge.

"Then you wouldn't like Dr. Breen for a daughter," returned her son, in the same tone as before.

"She wouldn't like me for a mother," Mrs. Mulbridge retorted. Her son laughed, and helped himself to more baked beans and a fresh slice of rye-and-Indian. He had the homely tastes and the strong digestion of the people from whom he sprung; and he handed his cup to be filled with his mother's strong coffee in easy defiance of consequences. As he took it back from her he said, "I should like to see you and Mrs. Breen together. You would make a strong team." He buttered his bread, with another laugh in appreciation of his conceit. "If you happened to pull the same way. If you didn't, something would break. Mrs. Breen is a lady of powerful convictions. She thinks you ought to be good, and you ought to be very sorry for it, but not so sorry as you ought to be for being happy. I don't think she has given her daughter any reason to complain on the last score." He broke into his laugh again, and watched his mother's frown with interest. "I suspect that she doesn't like me very well. You could meet on common ground there: you don't like her daughter."

"They must be a pair of them," said Mrs. Mulbridge immovably. "Did her mother like her studying for a doctor?"

"Yes, I understand so. Her mother is progressive she believes in the advancement of women; she thinks the men would oppress them if they got a chance."

"If one half the bold things that are running about the country had masters it would be the best thing," said Mrs. Mulbridge, opening the lid of the coffee-pot, and clapping it to with force, after a glance inside.

"That's where Mrs. Green wouldn't agree with you. Perhaps because it would make the bold things happy to have masters, though she doesn't say so. Probably she wants the women to have women doctors so they won't be so well, and can have more time to think whether they have been good or not. You ought to hear some of the ladies over there talk, mother."

"I have heard enough of their talk."

"Well, you ought to hear Miss Gleason. There are very few things that Miss Gleason doesn't think can be done with cut flowers, from a wedding to a funeral."

Mrs. Mulbridge perceived that her son was speaking figuratively of Miss Gleason's sentimentality, but she was not very patient with the sketch he, enjoyed giving of her. "Is she a friend of that Breen girl's?" she interrupted to ask.

"She's an humble friend, an admirer, a worshipper. The Breen girl is her ideal woman. She thinks the Breen girl is so superior to any man living that she would like to make a match for her." His mother glanced sharply at him, but he went on in the tone of easy generalization, and with a certain pleasure in the projection of these strange figures against her distorting imagination: "You see, mother, that the most advanced thinkers among those ladies are not so very different, after all, from you old-fashioned people. When they try to think of the greatest good fortune that can befall an ideal woman, it is to have her married. The only trouble is to find a man good enough; and if they can't find one, they're apt to invent one. They have strong imaginations."

"I should think they would make you sick, amongst them," said his mother. "Are you going to have anything more to eat?" she asked, with a housekeeper's latent impatience to get her table cleared away.

"Yes," said Dr. Mulbridge; "I haven't finished yet. And I'm in no hurry this morning. Sit still, mother; I want you to hear something more about my lady friends at Jocelyn's. Dr. Breen's mother and Miss Gleason don't feel alike about her. Her mother thinks she was weak in giving up Mrs. Maynard's case to me; but Miss Gleason told me about their discussion, and she thinks it is the great heroic act of Dr. Breen's life."

"It showed some sense, at least," Mrs. Mulbridge replied. She had tacitly offered to release her son from telling her anything when she had made her motion to rise; if he chose to go on now, it was his own affair. She handed him the plate of biscuit, and he took one.

"It showed inspiration, Miss Gleason says. The tears came into her eyes; I understood her to say it was godlike. 'And only to think, doctor,'" he continued, with a clumsy, but unmistakable suggestion of Miss Gleason's perfervid manner, "'that such a girl should be dragged down by her own mother to the level of petty, every-day cares and duties, and should be blamed for the most beautiful act of self-sacrifice! Isn't it too bad?'"

"Rufus, Rufus!" cried his mother, "I can't stun' it! Stop!"

"Oh, Dr. Breen isn't so bad - not half so divine as Miss Gleason thinks her. And Mrs. Maynard doesn't consider her surrendering the case an act of self-sacrifice at all."

"I should hope not!" said Mrs. Mulbridge. "I guess she wouldn't have been alive to tell the tale, if it hadn't been for you."

"Oh, you can't be sure of that. You mustn't believe too much in doctors, mother. Mrs. Maynard is pretty tough. And she's had wonderfully good nursing. You've only heard the Barlow side of the matter," said her sun, betraying now for the first time that he had been aware of any knowledge of it on her part. That was their way: though they seldom told each other anything, and went on as if they knew nothing of each other's affairs, yet when they recognized this knowledge it was without surprise on either side. "I could tell you a different story. She's a very fine girl, mother; cool and careful under instruction, and perfectly tractable and intelligent. She's as different from those other women you've seen as you are. You would like her!" He had suddenly grown earnest, and crushing the crust of a biscuit in the strong left hand which he rested on the table, he gazed keenly at her undemonstrative face. "She's no baby, either. She's got a will and a temper of her own. She's the only one of them I ever saw that was worth her salt."

"I thought you didn't like self-willed women," said his mother impassively.

"She knows when to give up," he answered, with unrelaxed scrutiny.

His mother did not lift her eyes, yet. "How long shall you have to visit over there?"

"I've made my last professional visit."

"Where are you going this morning?"

"To Jocelyn's."

Mrs. Mulbridge now looked up, and met her son's eye. "What makes you think she'll have you?"

He did not shrink at her coming straight to the point the moment the way was clear. He had intended it, and he liked it. But he frowned a little as he said, "Because I want her to have me, for one thing." His jaw closed heavily, but his face lost a certain brutal look almost as quickly as it had assumed it. "I guess," he said, with a smile, "that it's the only reason I've got."

"You no need to say that," said his mother, resenting the implication that any woman would not have him.

"Oh, I'm not pretty to look at, mother, and I'm not particularly young; and for a while I thought there might be some one, else."

"Who?"

"The young fellow that came with her, that day."

"That whipper-snapper?"

Dr. Mulbridge assented by his silence. "But I guess I was mistaken. I guess he's tried and missed it. The field is 'clear, for all I can see. And she's made a failure in one way, and then you know a woman is in the humor to try it in another. She wants a good excuse for giving up. That's what I think."

"Well," said his mother, "I presume you know what you're about, Rufus!"

She took up the coffee-pot on the lid of which she had been keeping her hand, and went into the kitchen with it. She removed the dishes, and left him sitting before the empty table-cloth. When she came for that, he took hold of her hand, and looked up into her face, over which a scarcely discernible tremor passed. "Well, mother?"

"It's what I always knew I had got to come to, first or last. And I suppose I ought to feel glad enough I didn't have to come to it at first."

"No!" said her son. "I'm not a stripling any longer." He laughed, keeping his mother's hand.

She freed it and taking up the table-cloth folded it lengthwise and then across, and laid it neatly away in the cupboard. "I sha'n't interfere with you, nor any woman that you bring here to be your wife. I've had my day, and I'm not one of the old fools that think they're going to have and to hold forever. You've always been a good boy to me, and I guess you hain't ever had to complain' of your mother stan'in' in your way. I sha'n't now. But I did think - "

She stopped and shut her lips firmly. "Speak up, mother!" he cried.

"I guess I better not," she answered, setting her chair back against the wall.

"I know what you mean. You mean about my laughing at

women that try to take men's places in the world. Well, I did laugh at them. They're ridiculous. I don't want to marry this girl because she's a doctor. That was the principal drawback, in my mind. But it doesn't make any difference, and wouldn't now, if she was a dozen doctors."

His mother let down the leaves of the table, and pushed it against the wall, and he rose from the chair in which he was left sitting in the middle of the room. "I presume," she said, with her back toward him, as she straightened the table accurately against the mopboard, "that you can let me have the little house at Grant's Corner."

"Why, mother!" he cried. "You don't suppose I should ever let you be turned out of house and home? You can stay here as long as you live. But it hasn't come to that, yet. I don't know that she cares anything about me. But there are chances, and there are signs. The chances are that she won't have the courage to take up her plan of life again, and that she'll consider any other that's pressed home upon her. And I take it for a good sign that she's sent that fellow adrift. If her mind hadn't been set on some one else, she'd have taken him, in this broken-up state of hers. Besides, she has formed the habit of doing what I say, and there's a great deal in mere continuity of habit. It will be easier for her to say yes than to say no; it would be very hard for her to say no."

While he eagerly pressed these arguments his mother listened stonily, without apparent interest or sympathy. But at the end she asked, "How are you going to support a wife? Your practice here won't do it. Has she got anything?"

"She has property, I believe," replied her son. "She seems to have been brought up in that way."

"She won't want to come and live here, then. She'll have notions of her own. If she's like the rest of them, she'll never have you."

"If she were like the rest of them, I'd never have her. But she isn't. As far as I'm concerned, it's nothing against her that she's studied medicine. She didn't do it from vanity, or ambition, or any abnormal love of it. She did it, so far so I can find out, because she wished to do good that way. She's been a little notional, she's had her head addled by women's talk, and she's in a queer freak; but it's only a girl's freak after all: you can't say anything worse of her. She's a splendid woman, and her property's neither here nor there. I could support her."

"I presume," replied his mother, "that she's been used to ways that ain't like our ways. I've always stuck up for you, Rufus, stiff enough, I guess; but I ain't agoin' to deny that you're country born and bred. I can see that, and she can see it, too. It makes a great difference with girls. I don't know as she'd call you what they call a gentleman."

Dr. Mulbridge flushed angrily. Every American, of whatever standing or breeding, thinks of himself as a gentleman, and nothing can gall him more than the insinuation that he is less. "What do you mean, mother?"

"You hain't ever been in such ladies' society as hers in the same way. I know that they all think the world of you, and flatter you up, and they're as biddable as you please when you're doctorin' 'em; but I guess it would be different if you was to set up for one of their own kind amongst 'em."

"There isn't one of them," he retorted, "that I don't believe I could have for the turn of my hand, especially if it was doubled into a fist. They like force."

"Oh, you've only seen the sick married ones. I guess you'll find a well girl is another thing."

"They're all alike. And I think I should be something of a relief if I wasn't like what she's been used to hearing called a gentleman; she'd prefer me on that account. But if you come to blood, I guess the Mulbridges and Gardiner, can hold up their heads with the best, anywhere."

"Yes, like the Camfers and Rafllins." These were people of ancestral consequence and local history, who had gone up to Boston from Corbitant, and had succeeded severally as green-grocers and retail dry-goods men, with the naturally attendant social distinction.

"Pshaw!" cried her son. "If she cares for me at all, she won't care for the cut of my clothes, or my table manners."

"Yes, that's so. 'T ain't on my account that I want you should make sure she doos care."

He looked hard at her immovable face, with its fallen eyes, and then went out of the room. He never quarrelled with his mother, because his anger, like her own, was dumb, and silenced him as it mounted. Her misgivings had stung him deeply, and at the bottom of his indolence and indifference was a fiery pride, not easily kindled, but unquenchable. He flung the harness upon his old unkempt horse, and tackled him to the mud-encrusted buggy, for whose shabbiness he had never cared before. He was tempted to go back into the house, and change his uncouth Canada homespun coat for the broadcloth frock which he wore when he went to Boston; but he scornfully resisted it, and drove off in his accustomed figure.

His mother's last words repeated themselves to him, and in that dialogue, in which he continued to dramatize their different feelings, he kept replying, "Well, the way to find out whether she cares is to ask her."

X

During her convalescence Mrs. Maynard had the time and inclination to give Grace some good advice. She said that she had thought a great deal about it throughout her sickness, and she had come to the conclusion that Grace was throwing away her life.

"You're not fit to be a doctor, Grace," she said. "You're too nervous, and you're too conscientious. It isn't merely your want of experience. No matter how much experience you had, if you saw a case going wrong in your hands, you'd want to call in some one else to set it right. Do you suppose Dr. Mulbridge would have given me up to another doctor because he was afraid he couldn't cure me? No, indeed! He'd have let me die first, and I shouldn't have blamed him. Of course I know what pressure I brought to bear upon you, but you had no business to mind me. You oughtn't to have minded my talk any more than the buzzing of a mosquito, and no real doctor would. If he wants to be a success, he must be hard-hearted; as hard-hearted as" - she paused for a comparison, and failing any other added - "as all possessed." To the like large-minded and impartial effect, she, ran on at great length. "No, Grace," she concluded, "what you want to do is to get married. You would be a good wife, and you would be a good mother. The only trouble is that I don't know any man worthy of you, or half worthy. No, I don't!"

Now that her recovery was assured, Mrs. Maynard was very forgiving and sweet and kind with every one. The ladies who came in to talk with her said that she was a changed creature; she gave them all the best advice, and she had absolutely no shame whatever for the inconsistency involved by her reconciliation with her husband. She rather flaunted the happiness of her reunion in the face of the public, and she vouchsafed an explanation to no one. There had never been anything definite in her charges against him, even to Grace, and her tacit withdrawal of them succeeded perfectly well. The ladies, after some cynical tittering, forgot them, and rejoiced in the spectacle of conjugal harmony afforded them: women are generous creatures, and there is hardly any offence which they are not willing another woman should forgive her husband, when once they have said that they do not see how she could ever forgive him.

Mrs. Maynard's silence seemed insufficient to none but Mrs. Breen and her own husband. The former vigorously denounced its want of logic to Grace as all but criminal, though she had no objection to Mr. Maynard. He, in fact, treated her with a filial respect which went far to efface her preconceptions; and he did what he could to retrieve himself from the disgrace of a separation in Grace's eyes. Perhaps he thought that the late situation was known to her alone, when he casually suggested, one day, that Mrs. Maynard was peculiar.

"Yes," said Grace mercifully; "but she has been out of health so long. That makes a great difference. She's going to be better now."

"Oh, it's going to come out all right in the end," he said, with his unbuoyant hopefulness, "and I reckon I've got to help it along. Why, I suppose every man's a trial at times, doctor?"

"I dare say. I know that every woman is," said the girl.

"Is that so? Well, may be you're partly right. But you don't suppose but what a man generally begins it, do you? There was Adam, you know. He didn't pull the apple; but he fell off into that sleep, and woke up with one of his ribs dislocated, and

William Dean Howells

that's what really commenced the trouble. If it hadn't been for Adam, there wouldn't have been any woman, you know; and you couldn't blame her for what happened after she got going?" There was no gleam of insinuation in his melancholy eye, and Grace listened without quite knowing what to make of it all. "And then I suppose he wasn't punctual at meals, and stood round talking politics at night, when he ought to have been at home with his family?"

"Who?" asked Grace.

"Adam," replied Mr. Maynard lifelessly. "Well, they got along pretty well outside," he continued. "Some of the children didn't turn out just what you might have expected; but raising children is mighty uncertain business. Yes, they got along." He ended his parable with a sort of weary sigh, as if oppressed by experience. Grace looked at his slovenly figure, his smoky complexion, and the shaggy outline made by his untrimmed hair and beard, and she wondered how Louise could marry him; but she liked him, and she was willing to accept for all reason the cause of unhappiness at which he further hinted. "You see, doctor, an incompatibility is a pretty hard thing to manage. You can't forgive it like a real grievance. You have to try other things, and find out that there are worse things, and then you come back to it and stand it. We're talking Wyoming and cattle range, now, and Mrs. Maynard is all for the new deal; it's going to make us healthy, wealthy, and wise. Well, I suppose the air will be good for her, out there. You doctors are sending lots of your patients our way, now." The gravity with which he always assumed that Grace was a physician in full and regular practice would have had its edge of satire, coming from another; but from him, if it was ironical, it was also caressing, and she did not resent it. "I've had some talk with your colleague, here, Dr. Mulbridge, and he seems to think it will be the best thing for her. I suppose you agree with him?"

"Oh, yes," said Grace, "his opinion would be of great value. It wouldn't be at all essential that I should agree with him:'

"Well, I don't know about that," said Maynard. "I reckon he thinks a good deal of your agreeing with him. I've been talking with him about settling out our way. We've got a magnificent country, and there's bound to be plenty of sickness there, sooner or later. Why, doctor, it would be a good opening for you! It's just the place for you. You're off here in a corner, in New England, and you haven't got any sort of scope; but at Cheyenne you'd have the whole field to yourself; there isn't another lady doctor in Cheyenne. Now, you come out with us. Bring your mother with you, and grow up with the country. Your mother would like it. There's enough moral obliquity in Cheyenne to keep her conscience in a state of healthful activity all the time. Yes, you'd get along out there."

Grace laughed, and shook her head. It was part of the joke which life seemed to be with Mr. Maynard that the inhabitants of New England were all eager to escape from their native section, and that they ought to be pitied and abetted in this desire. As soon as his wife's convalescence released him from constant attendance upon her, he began an inspection of the region from the compassionate point of view; the small, frugal husbandry appealed to his commiseration, and he professed to have found the use of canvas caps upon the haycocks intolerably pathetic. "Why, I'm told," he said, "that they have to blanket the apple-trees while the fruit is setting; and they kill off our Colorado bugs by turning them loose, one at a time, on the potato-patches: the bug starves to death in forty-eight hours. But you've got plenty of schoolhouses, doctor; it does beat all, about the schoolhouses. And it's an awful pity that there are no children to go to school in them. Why, of course the people go West as fast as they can, but they ought to be helped; the Government ought to do something. They're good people; make first-rate citizens when you get them waked up, out there. But they ought all to be got away, and let somebody run New England' as a summer resort. It's pretty, and it's cool and pleasant, and the fishing is excellent; milk, eggs, and all kinds of berries and historical associations on the premises; and it could be made very attractive three months of the year; but my goodness! you oughtn't to ask anybody to live here. You come out with us, doctor, and see that country, and you'll know what I mean."

His boasts were always uttered with a wan, lack-lustre irony, as if he were burlesquing the conventional Western brag and enjoying the mystifications of his listener, whose feeble sense of humor often failed to seize his intention, and to whom any depreciation of New England was naturally unintelligible. She had not come to her final liking for him without a season of serious misgiving, but after that she rested in peace upon what every one knowing him felt to be his essential neighborliness. Her wonder had then come to be how he could marry Louise, when they sat together on the seaward piazza, and he poured out his easy talk, unwearied and unwearying, while, with one long, lank leg crossed upon the other, he swung his unblacked, thin-soled boot to and fro.

"Well, he was this kind of a fellow: When we were in Switzerland, he was always climbing some mountain or other. They couldn't have hired me to climb one of their mountains if they'd given me all their scenery, and thrown their goitres in. I used to tell him that the side of a house was good enough for me. But nothing but the tallest mountains would do him; and one day when he was up there on the comb of the roof somewhere, tied with a rope round his waist to the guide and a Frenchman, the guide's foot slipped, and he commenced going down. The Frenchman was just going to cut the rope and let the guide play it alone; but he knocked the knife out of his hand with his long-handled axe, and when the jerk came he was on the other side of the comb, where he could brace himself, and brought them both up standing. Well, he's got muscles like bunches of steel wire. Didn't he ever tell you about it?"

"No," said Grace sadly.

"Well, somebody ought to expose Libby. I don't suppose I should ever have known about it myself, if I hadn't happened to see the guide's friends and relations crying over him next

day as if he was the guide's funeral. Hello! There's the doctor."
He unlimbered his lank legs, and rose with an effect of
opening his person like a pocket-knife. "As I understand it,
this is an unprofessional visit, and the doctor is here among us
as a guest. I don't know exactly what to do under the
circumstances, whether we ought to talk about Mrs. Maynard's
health or the opera; but I reckon if we show our good
intentions it will come out all right in the end."

He went forward to meet the doctor, who came up to shake
hands with Grace, and then followed him in-doors to see Mrs.
Maynard. Grace remained in her place, and she was still sitting
there when Dr. Mulbridge returned without him. He came
directly to her, and said, "I want to speak with you, Miss
Breen. Can I see you alone?"

"Is - is Mrs. Maynard worse?" she asked, rising in a little
trepidation.

"No; it has nothing to do with her. She's practically well now;
I can remand the case to you. I wish to see you - about
yourself." She hesitated at this peculiar summons, but some
pressure was upon her to obey Dr. Mulbridge, as there was
upon most people where he wished to obey him. "I want to
talk with you," he added, "about what you are going to do, -
about your future. Will you come?"

"Oh, yes," she answered; and she suffered him to lead the way
down from the piazza, and out upon one of the sandy avenues
toward the woods, in which it presently lost itself. "But there
will be very little to talk about," she continued, as they moved
away, "if you confine yourself to my future. I have none."

"I don't see how you've got rid of it," he rejoined. "You've got
a future as much as you have a past, and there's this advantage,
- that you can do something with your future."

"Do you think so?" she asked, with a little bitterness. "That
hasn't been my experience."

William Dean Howells

"It's been mine," he said, "and you can make it yours. Come, I want to talk with you about your future, because I have been thinking very seriously about my own. I want to ask your advice and to give you mine. I'll commence by asking yours. What do you think of me as a physician? I know you are able to judge."

She was flattered, in spite of herself. There were long arrears of cool indifference to her own claims in that direction, which she might very well have resented; but she did not. There was that flattery in his question which the junior in any vocation feels in the appeal of his senior; and there was the flattery which any woman feels in a man's recourse to her judgment. Still, she contrived to parry it with a little thrust. "I don't suppose the opinion of a mere homoeopathist can be of any value to a regular practitioner."

He laughed. "You have been a regular practitioner yourself for the last three weeks. What do you think of my management of the case?"

"I have never abandoned my principles," she began.

"Oh, I know all about that? What do you think of me as a doctor?" he persisted.

"Of course I admire you. Why do you ask me that?"

"Because I wished to know. And because I wished to ask you something else. You have been brought up in a city, and I have always lived here in the country, except the two years I was out with the army. Do you think I should succeed if I pulled up here, and settled in Boston?"

"I have not lived in Boston," she answered. "My opinion wouldn't be worth much on that point."

"Yes, it would. You know city people, and what they are. I have seen a good deal of them in my practice at the hotels about here, and some of the ladies - when they happened to feel more comfortable - have advised me to come to Boston." His derision seemed to throw contempt on all her sex; but he turned to her, and asked again earnestly, "What do you think? Some of the profession know me there. When I left the school, some of the faculty urged me to try my chance in the city."

She waited a moment before she answered. "You know that I must respect your skill, and I believe that you could succeed anywhere. I judge your fitness by my own deficiency. The first time I saw you with Mrs. Maynard, I saw that you had everything that I hadn't. I saw that I was a failure, and why, and that it would be foolish for me to keep up the struggle."

"Do you mean that you have given it up?" he demanded, with a triumph in which there was no sympathy.

"It has given me up. I never liked it, - I told you that before, - and I never took it up from any ambitious motive. It seemed a shame for me to be of no use in the world; and I hoped that I might do something in a way that seemed natural for women. And I don't give up because I'm unfit as a woman. I might be a man, and still be impulsive and timid and nervous, and everything that I thought I was not."

"Yes, you might be all that, and be a man; but you'd be an exceptional man, and I don't think you're an exceptional woman. If you've failed, it isn't your temperament that's to blame."

"I think it is. The wrong is somewhere in me individually. I know it is."

Dr. Mulbridge, walking beside her, with his hands clasped behind him, threw up his head and laughed. "Well, have it your own way, Miss Breen. Only I don't agree with you. Why should you wish to spare your sex at your own expense? But that's the way with some ladies, I've noticed. They approve of what women attempt because women attempt it, and they believe the attempt reflects honor on them. It's tremendous to think what men could accomplish for their sex, if they only hung together as women do. But they can't. They haven't the generosity."

"I think you don't understand me," said Grace, with a severity that amused him. "I wished to regard myself, in taking up this profession, entirely as I believed a man would have regarded himself."

"And were you able to do it?"

"No," she unintentionally replied to this unexpected question.

"Haw, haw, haw!" laughed Dr. Mulbridge at her helpless candor. "And are you sure that you give it up as a man would?"

"I don't know how you mean," she said, vexed and bewildered.

"Do you do it fairly and squarely because you believe that you're a failure, or because you partly feel that you haven't been fairly dealt with?"

"I believe that if Mrs. Maynard had had the same confidence in me that she would have had in any man I should not have failed. But every woman physician has a double disadvantage that I hadn't the strength to overcome, - her own inexperience and the distrust of other women."

"Well, whose fault is that?"

"Not the men's. It is the men alone who give women any chance. They are kind and generous and liberal-minded. I have no blame for them, and I have no patience with women who want to treat them as the enemies of women's advancement. Women can't move a step forwards without their sufferance and help. Dr. Mulbridge," she cried, "I wish to apologize for the hasty and silly words I used to you the day I came to ask you to consult with me. I ought to have been grateful to you for consenting at first, and when you took back your consent I ought to have considered your position. You were entirely right. We had no common ground to meet on, and I behaved like a petulant, foolish, vulgar girl!"

"No, no," he protested, laughing in recollection of the scene. "You were all right, and I was in a fix; and if your own fears hadn't come to the rescue, I don't know how I should have got out of it. It would have been disgraceful, wouldn't it, to refuse a lady's request. You don't know how near I was to giving way. I can tell you, now that it's all over. I had never seen a lady of our profession before," he added hastily, "and my curiosity was up. I always had my doubts about the thoroughness of women's study, and I should have liked to see where your training failed. I must say I found it very good, - I've told you that. You wouldn't fail individually: you would fail because you are a woman."

"I don't believe that," said Grace.

"Well, then, because your patients are women. It's all one. What will you do?"

"I shall not do anything. I shall give it all up."

"But what shall you do then?"

"I - don't know."

"What are you going to be? A fashionable woman? Or are you going to Europe, and settle down there with the other American failures? I've heard about them, - in Rome and Florence and Paris. Are you going to throw away the study you've put into this profession? You took it up because you wanted to do good. Don't you want to do good any more? Has the human race turned out unworthy?"

She cowered at this arraignment, in which she could not separate the mocking from the justice. "What do you advise

William Dean Howells

me to do? Do you think I could ever succeed?"

"You could never succeed alone."

"Yes, I know that; I felt that from the first. But I have planned to unite with a woman physician older than myself."

"And double your deficiency. Sit down here," he said; "I wish to talk business." They had entered the border of the woods encompassing Jocelyn's, and he painted to a stump, beside which lay the fallen tree. She obeyed mechanically, and he remained standing near her, with one foot lifted to the log; he leaned forward over her, and seemed to seize a physical advantage in the posture. "From your own point of view, you would have no right to give up your undertaking if there was a chance of success in it. You would have no more right to give up than a woman who had gone out as a missionary."

"I don't pretend to compare myself with such a woman; but I should have no more right to give up," she answered, helpless against the logic of her fate, which he had somehow divined.

"Well, then, listen to me. I can give you this chance. Are you satisfied that with my advice you could have succeeded in Mrs. Maynard's case?"

"Yes, I think so. But what" -

"I think so, too. Don't rise!"

His will overcame the impulse that had betrayed itself, and she sank back to her seat. "I offer you my advice from this time forward; I offer you my help."

"That is very good of you," she murmured; "and I appreciate your generosity more than I can say. I know the prejudice you must have had to overcome in regard to women physicians before you could bring yourself to do this; and I know how you must have despised me for failing in my attempt, and giving myself up to my feeble temperament. But" -

"Oh, we won't speak of all that," he interrupted. "Of course I felt the prejudice against women entering the profession which we all feel; it was ridiculous and disgusting to me till I saw you. I won't urge you from any personal motive to accept my offer. But I know that if you do you can realize all your hopes of usefulness; and I ask you to consider that certainly. But you know the only way it could be done."

She looked him in the eyes, with dismay in her growing intelligence.

"What - what do you mean?"

"I mean that I ask you to let me help you carry out your plan of life, and to save all you have done, and all you have hoped, from waste - as your husband. Think" -

She struggled to her feet as if he were opposing a palpable resistance, so strongly she felt the pressure of his will. "It can't be, Dr. Mulbridge. Oh, it can't, indeed! Let us go back; I wish to go back!"

But he had planted himself in her way, and blocked her advance, unless she chose to make it a flight.

"I expected this," he said, with a smile, as if her wild trepidation interested him as an anticipated symptom. "The whole idea is new and startling to you. But I know you won't dismiss it abruptly, and I won't be discouraged."

"Yes, yes, you must! I will not think of it! I can't! I do dismiss it at once. Let me go!"

"Then you really choose to be like the rest, - a thing of hysterical impulses, without conscience or reason! I supposed the weakest woman would be equal to an offer of marriage. And you had dreamt of being a physician and useful!"

162   William Dean Howells

"I tell you," she cried, half quelled by his derision, "that I have found out that I am not fit for it, - that I am a failure and a disgrace; and you had no right to expect me to be anything else."

"You are no failure, and I had a right to expect anything of you after the endurance and the discretion you have shown in the last three weeks. Without your help I should have failed myself. You owe it to other women to go on."

"They must take care of themselves," she said. "If my weakness throws shame on them, they must bear it. I thank you for what you say. I believe you mean it. But if I was of any use to you I didn't know it."

"It was probably inspiration, then," he interrupted coolly. "Come, this isn't a thing to be frightened at. You're not obliged to do what I say. But I think you ought to hear me out. I haven't spoken without serious thought, and I didn't suppose you would reject me without a reason."

"Reason?" she repeated. "There is no reason in it."

"There ought to be. There is, on my side. I have all kinds of reasons for asking you to be my wife: I believe that I can make you happy in the fulfilment of your plans; I admire you and respect you more than any other woman I ever saw; and I love you."

"I don't love you, and that is reason enough."

"Yes, between boys and girls. But between men and women it isn't enough. Do you dislike me?"

"No."

"Am I repulsive in any way?"

"No, no!"

"I know that I am not very young and that I am not very good-looking."

"It isn't that at all."

"Of course I know that such things weigh with women, and that personal traits and habits are important in an affair like this. I am slovenly and indifferent about my dress; but it's only because I have lived where every sort of spirit and ambition was useless. I don't know about city ways, but I could pick up all of them that were worth while. I spoke of going to Boston; but I would go anywhere else with you, east or west, that you chose, and I know that I should succeed. I haven't done what I might have done with myself, because I've never had an object in life. I've always lived in the one little place, and I've never been out of it except when I was in the army. I've always liked my profession; but nothing has secmed worth while. You were a revelation to me; you have put ambition and hope into me. I never saw any woman before that I would have turned my hand to have. They always seemed to me fit to be the companions of fools, or the playthings of men. But of all the simpletons, the women who were trying to do something for woman, as they called it, trying to exemplify and illustrate a cause, were the silliest that I came across. I never happened to have met a woman doctor before you came to me; but I had imagined them, and I couldn't believe in you when I saw you. You were not supersensitive, you were not presumptuous, and you gave up, not because you distrusted yourself, but because your patient distrusted you. That was right: I should have done the same thing myself. Under my direction, you have shown yourself faithful, docile, patient, intelligent beyond anything I have seen. I have watched you, and I know; and I know what your peculiar trials have been from that woman. You have taught me a lesson, - I 'm not ashamed to say it; and you've given me a motive. I was wrong to ask you to marry me so that you might carry out your plans: that was no way to appeal to you. What I meant was that I might make your plans my own, and that we might carry them out together. I don't care for making money; I have always been poor, and I had always

William Dean Howells

expected to be so; and I am not afraid of hard work. There isn't any self-sacrifice you've dreamed of that I wouldn't gladly and proudly share with you. You can't do anything by yourself, but we could do anything together. If you have any scruple about giving up your theory of medicine, you needn't do it; and the State Medical Association may go to the devil. I've said my say. What do you say?"

She looked all round, as if seeking escape from a mesh suddenly flung about her, and then she looked imploringly up at him. "I have nothing to say," she whispered huskily. "I can't answer you."

"Well, that's all I ask," he said, moving a few steps, away, and suffering her to rise. "Don't answer me now. Take time, - all the time you want, all the time there is."

"No," she said, rising, and gathering some strength from the sense of being on foot again. "I don't mean that. I mean that I don't - I can't consent."

"You don't believe in me? You don't think I would do it?"

"I don't believe in myself. I have no right to doubt you. I know that I ought to honor you for what you propose."

"I don't think it calls for any great honor. Of course I shouldn't propose it to every lady physician." He smiled with entire serenity and self-possession. "Tell me one thing: was there ever a time when you would have consented?" She did not answer. "Then you will consent yet?"

"No. Don't deceive yourself. I shall never consent."

"I'll leave that to the logic of your own conscience. You will do what seems your duty."

"You mustn't trust to my conscience. I fling it away! I won't have anything to do with it. I've been tortured enough by it.

There is no sense or justice in it!"

He laughed easily at her vehemence. "I'll trust your conscience. But I won't stay to worry you now. I'm coming again day after to-morrow, and I'm not afraid of what you will say then."

He turned and left her, tearing his way through the sweet-fern and low blackberry vines, with long strides, a shape of uncouth force. After he was out of sight, she followed, scared and trembling at herself, as if she had blasphemed.

XI

Grace burst into the room where her mother sat; and flung her hat aside with a desperate gesture. "Now, mother, you have got to listen to me. Dr. Mulbridge has asked me to marry him!"

Mrs. Green put up her spectacles on her forehead, and stared at her daughter, while some strong expressions, out of the plebeian or rustic past which lies only a generation or two behind most of us, rose to her lips. I will not repeat them here; she had long denied them to herself as an immoral self-indulgence, and it must be owned that such things have a fearful effect, coming from old ladies. "What has got into all the men? What in nature does he want you to marry him for?"

"Oh, for the best reasons in the world," exclaimed the daughter. "For reasons that will make you admire and respect him," she added ironically. "For great, and unselfish, and magnanimous reasons!"

"I should want to believe they were the real ones, first," interrupted Mrs. Breen.

"He wants to marry me because he knows that I can't fulfil my plans of life alone, and because we could fulfil them together. We shall not only be husband and wife, but we shall be physicians in partnership. I may continue a homoeopath, he says, and the State Medical Association may go to the devil." She used his language, that would have been shocking to her ordinary moods, without blenching, and in their common agitation her mother accepted it as fit and becoming. "He counts upon my accepting him because I must see it as my duty, and my conscience won't let me reject the only opportunity I shall have of doing some good and being of some use in the world. What do you think I ought to do, mother?"

"There's reason in what he says. It is an opportunity. You could be of use, in that way, and perhaps it's the only way. Yes," she continued, fascinated by the logic of the position, and its capabilities for vicarious self-sacrifice. "I don't see how you can get out of it: You have spent years and years of study, and a great deal of money, to educate yourself for a profession that you're too weak to practise alone. You can't say that I ever advised your doing it. It was your own idea, and I didn't oppose it. But when you've gone so far, you've formed an obligation to go on. It's your duty not to give up, if you know of any means to continue. That's your duty, as plain as can be. To say nothing of the wicked waste of your giving up now, you're bound to consider the effect it would have upon other women who are trying to do something for themselves. The only thing," she added, with some misgiving, "is whether you believe he was in earnest and would keep his word to you."

"I think he was secretly laughing at me, and that he would expect to laugh me out of his promise."

"Well, then, you ought to take time to reflect, and you ought to be sure that you're right about him."

"Is that what you really think, mother?"

"I am always governed by reason, Grace, and by right; and I have brought you up on that plan. If you have ever departed from it, it has not been with my consent, nor for want of my warning. I have simply laid the matter before you."

"Then you wish me to marry him?"

This was perhaps a point that had not occurred to Mrs. Breen in her recognition of the strength of Dr. Mulbridge's position. It was one thing to trace the path of duty; another to support the aspirant in treading it. "You ought to take time to reflect," Mrs. Green repeated, with evasion that she never used in behalf of others.

"Well, mother," answered Grace, "I didn't take time to reflect, and I shouldn't care whether I was right about him or not. I refused him because I didn't love him. If I had loved him that would have been the only reason I needed to marry him. But all the duty in the world wouldn't be enough without it. Duty? I am sick of duty! Let the other women who are trying to do something for themselves, take care of themselves as men would. I don't owe them more than a man would owe other men, and I won't be hoodwinked into thinking I do. As for the waste, the past is gone, at any rate; and the waste that I lament is the years I spent in working myself up to an undertaking that I was never fit for. I won't continue that waste, and I won't keep up the delusion that because I was very unhappy I was useful, and that it was doing good to be miserable. I like pleasure and I like dress; I like pretty things. There is no harm in them. Why shouldn't I have them?"

"There is harm in them for you," - her mother began.

"Because I have tried to make my life a horror? There is no other reason, and that is no reason. When we go into Boston this winter I shall go to the theatre. I shall go to the opera, and I hope there will be a ballet. And next summer, I am going to Europe; I am going to Italy." She whirled away toward the door as if she were setting out.

"I should think you had taken leave of your conscience!" cried her mother.

"I hope I have, mother. I am going to consult my reason after this."

"Your reason!"

"Well, then, my inclination. I have had enough of conscience, - of my own, and of yours, too. That is what I told him, and that is what I mean. There is such a thing as having too much conscience, and of getting stupefied by it, so that you can't really see what's right. But I don't care. I believe I should like to do wrong for a while, and I will do wrong if it's doing right to marry him."

She had her hand on the door-knob, and now she opened the door, and closed it after her with something very like a bang.

She naturally could not keep within doors in this explosive state, and she went downstairs, and out upon the piazza. Mr. Maynard was there, smoking, with his boots on top of the veranda-rail, and his person thrown back in his chair at the angle requisite to accomplish this elevation of the feet. He took them down, as he saw her approach, and rose, with the respect in which he never failed for women, and threw his cigar away.

"Mr. Maynard," she asked abruptly, "do you know where Mr. Libby is?"

"No, I don't, doctor, I'm sorry to say. If I did, I would send and borrow some more cigars of him. I think that the brand our landlord keeps must have been invented by Mr. Track, the great anti-tobacco reformer."

"Is he coming back? Isn't he coming back?" she demanded breathlessly.

"Why, yes, I reckon he must be coming back. Libby generally sees his friends through. And he'll have some curiosity to know how Mrs. Maynard and I have come out of it all." He looked at her with something latent in his eye; but what his eye expressed was merely a sympathetic regret that he could not be more satisfactory.

"Perhaps," she suggested, "Mr. Barlow might know something."

"Well, now," said Maynard, "perhaps he might, that very thing. I'll go round and ask him." He went to the stable, and she waited for his return. "Barlow says," he reported, "that he guesses he's somewhere about Leyden. At any rate, his mare,'s there yet, in the stable where Barlow left her. He saw her there, yesterday."

"Thanks. That's all I wished to know," said Grace. "I wished to write to him," she added boldly.

She shut herself in her room and spent the rest of the forenoon in writing a letter, which when first finished was very long, but in its ultimate phase was so short as to occupy but a small space on a square correspondence-card. Having got it written on the card, she was dissatisfied with it in that shape, and copied it upon a sheet of note-paper. Then she sealed and addressed it, and put it into her pocket; after dinner she went down to the beach, and walked a long way upon the sands. She thought at first that she would ask Barlow to get it to him, somehow; and then she determined to find out from Barlow the address of the people who had Mr. Libby's horse, and send it to them for him by the driver of the barge. She would approach the driver with a nonchalant, imperious air, and ask him to please have that delivered to Mr. Libby immediately; and in case he learned from the stable-people that he was not in Leyden, to bring the letter back to her. She saw how the driver would take it, and then she figured Libby opening and reading it. She sometimes figured him one way, and sometimes another. Sometimes he rapidly scanned the lines, and then instantly ordered his horse, and feverishly hastened the men; again he deliberately read it, and then tore it into stall pieces, with a laugh, and flung them away. This conception of his behavior made her heart almost stop beating; but there was a luxury in it, too, and she recurred to it quite as often as to the other, which led her to a dramatization of their meeting, with all their parley minutely realized, and every most intimate look and thought imagined. There is of course no means of proving that this sort of mental exercise was in any degree an exercise of the reason, or that Dr. Breen did not behave unprofessionally in giving herself up to it. She could only have claimed in self-defence that she was no longer aiming at a professional behavior; that she was in fact abandoning herself to a recovered sense of girlhood and all its sweetest irresponsibilities. Those who would excuse so weak and capricious a character may urge, if they like, that she was behaving as wisely as a young physician of the other sex would have done in the circumstances.

She concluded to remain on the beach, where only the children were playing in the sand, and where she could easily escape any other companionship that threatened. After she had walked long enough to spend the first passion of her reverie, she sat down under the cliff, and presently grew conscious of his boat swinging at anchor in its wonted place, and wondered that she had not thought he must come back for that. Then she had a mind to tear up her letter as superfluous; but she did not. She rose from her place under the cliff, and went to look for the dory. She found it drawn up on the sand in a little cove. It was the same place, and the water was so shoal for twenty feet out that no one could have rowed the dory to land; it must be dragged up. She laughed and blushed, and then boldly amused herself by looking for footprints; but the tide must have washed them out long ago; there were only the light, small footprints of the children who had been playing about the dory. She brushed away some sand they had scattered over the seat, and got into the boat and sat down there. It was a good seat, and commanded a view of the sail-boat in the foreground of the otherwise empty ocean; she took out her letter, and let it lie in the open hands which she let lie in her lap.

She was not impatient to have the time pass; it went only too soon. Though she indulged that luxury of terror in imagining her letter torn up and scornfully thrown away, she really rested quite safe as to the event; but she liked this fond delay, and the soft blue afternoon might have lasted forever to her entire content.

A little whiff of breeze stole up, and suddenly caught the letter from her open hands, and whisked it out over the sand. With a cry she fled after it, and when she had recaptured it, she thought to look at her watch. It was almost time for the barge, and now she made such needless haste, in order not to give herself chance for misgiving or retreat, that she arrived too soon at the point where she meant to intercept the driver on his way to the house; for in her present mutiny she had resolved to gratify a little natural liking for manoeuvre, long starved by the rigid discipline to which she had subjected herself. She had always been awkward at it, but she liked it; and now it pleased her to think that she should give her letter secretly to the driver, and on her way to meet him she forgot that she had meant to ask Barlow for part of the address. She did not remember this till it was too late to go back to the hotel, and she suddenly resolved not to consult Barlow, but to let the driver go about from one place to another with the letter till he found the right one. She kept walking on out into the forest through which the road wound, and she had got a mile away before she saw the weary bowing of the horses' heads as they tugged the barge through the sand at a walk. She stopped involuntarily, with some impulses to flight; and as the vehicle drew nearer, she saw the driver turned round upon his seat, and talking to a passenger behind. She had never counted upon his having a passenger, and the fact undid all.

She remained helpless in the middle of the road; the horses came to a stand-still a few paces from her, and the driver ceased from the high key of conversation, and turned to see what was the matter.

"My grief!" he shouted. "If it hadn't been for them horses o' mine, I sh'd 'a' run right over ye."

"I wished to speak with you," she began. "I wished to send" -

She stopped, and the passenger leaned forward to learn what was going on. "Miss Breen!" he exclaimed, and leaped out of the back of the barge and ran to her.

"You - you got my letter!" she gasped.

"No! What letter? Is there anything the matter?"

She did not answer. She had become conscious of the letter, which she had never ceased to hold in the hand that she had kept in her pocket for that purpose. She crushed it into a small wad.

Libby turned his head, and said to the driver of the barge, "Go ahead."

"Will you take my arm?" he added to her. "It's heavy walking in this sand."

"No, thank you," she murmured, recoiling. "I'm not tired."

"Are you well? Have you been quite well?"

"Oh, yes, perfectly. I didn't know you were coming back."

"Yes. I had to come back. I'm going to Europe next week, and I had to come to look after my boat, here; and I wanted to say good-by to Maynard. I was just going to speak to Maynard, and then sail my boat over to Leyden."

"It will be very pleasant," she said, without looking at him. "It's moonlight now."

"Oh, I sha'n't have any use for the moon. I shall get over before nightfall, if this breeze holds."

She tried to think of something else, and to get away from this talk of a sail to Leyden, but she fatally answered, "I saw your boat this afternoon. I hadn't noticed before that it was

William Dean Howells

still here."

He hesitated a moment, and then asked, "Did you happen to notice the dory?"

"Yes, it was drawn up on the sand."

"I suppose it's all right - if it's in the same place."

"It seemed to be," she answered faintly.

"I'm going to give the boat to Johnson."

She did not say anything, for she could think of nothing to say, but that she had looked for seals on the reef, but had not seen any, and this would have been too shamelessly leading. That left the word to him, and he asked timidly, -

"I hope my coming don't seem intrusive, Miss Breen?"

She did not heed this, but "You are going to be gone a great while?" she asked, in turn.

"I don't know," he replied, in an uncertain tone, as if troubled to make out whether she was vexed with him or not. "I thought," he added, "I would go up the Nile this time. I've never been up the Nile, you know."

"No, I didn't know that. Well," she added to herself, "I wish you had not come back! You had better not have come back. If you hadn't come, you would have got my letter. And now it can never be done! No, I can't go through it all again, and no one has the right to ask it. We have missed the only chance," she cried to herself, in such keen reproach of him that she thought she must have spoken aloud.

"Is Mrs. Maynard all right again?" he asked.

"Yes, she is very much better," she answered, confusedly, as if he had heard her reproach and had ignored it.

"I hope you're not so tired as you were."

"No, I'm not tired now."

"I thought you looked a little pale," he said sympathetically, and now she saw that he was so. It irritated her that she should be so far from him, in all helpfulness, and she could scarcely keep down the wish that ached in her heart.

We are never nearer doing the thing we long to do than when we have proclaimed to ourselves that it must not and cannot be.

"Why are you so pale?" she demanded, almost angrily.

"I? I didn't know that I was," he answered. "I supposed I was pretty well. I dare say I ought to be ashamed of showing it in that way. But if you ask me, well, I will tell you; I don't find it any easier than I did at first."

"You are to blame, then!" she cried. "If I were a man, I should not let such a thing wear upon me for a moment."

"Oh, I dare say I shall live through it," he answered, with the national whimsicality that comes to our aid in most emergencies.

A little pang went through her heart, but she retorted, "I wouldn't go to Europe to escape it, nor up the Nile. I would stay and fight it where I was." "Stay?" He seemed to have caught hopefully at the word.

"I thought you were stronger. If you give up in this way how can you expect me" - She stopped; she hardly knew what she had intended to say; she feared that he knew.

But he only said: "I'm sorry. I didn't intend to trouble you with the sight of me. I had a plan for getting over the cliff without letting you know, and having Maynard come down to me there."

"And did you really mean," she cried piteously, "to go away without trying to see me again?"

"Yes," he owned simply. "I thought I might catch a glimpse of you, but I didn't expect to speak to you."

"Did you hate me so badly as that? What had I done to you?"

"Done?" He gave a sorrowful laugh; and added, with an absent air, "Yes, it's really like doing something to me! And sometimes it seems as if you had done it purposely."

"You know I didn't! Now, then," she cried, "you have insulted me, and you never did that before. You were very good and noble and generous, and wouldn't let me blame myself for anything. I wanted always to remember that of you; for I didn't believe that any man could be so magnanimous. But it seems that you don't care to have me respect you!"

"Respect?" he repeated, in the same vague way. "No, I shouldn't care about that unless it was included in the other. But you know whether I have accused you of anything, or whether I have insulted you. I won't excuse myself. I think that ought to be insulting to your common sense."

"Then why should you have wished to avoid seeing me to-day? Was it to spare yourself?" she demanded, quite incoherently now. "Or did you think I should not be equal to the meeting?"

"I don't know what to say to you," answered the young man. "I think I must be crazy." He halted, and looked at her in complete bewilderment. "I don't understand you at all."

"I wished to see you very much. I wanted your advice, as - as - a friend." He shook his head. "Yes! you shall be my friend, in this at least. I can claim it - demand it. You had no right to - to - make me - trust you so much, and - and then - desert me."

"Oh, very well," he answered. "If any advice of mine - But I couldn't go through that sacrilegious farce of being near you and not" - She waited breathlessly, a condensed eternity, for him to go on; but he stopped at that word, and added: "How can I advise you?"

The disappointment was so cruel that the tears came into her eyes and ran down her face, which she averted from him. When she could control herself she said, "I have an opportunity of going on in my profession now, in a way that makes me sure of success."

"I am very glad on your account. You must be glad to realize"

"No, no!" she retorted wildly. "I am not glad!"

"I thought you" -

"But there are conditions! He says he will go with me anywhere, and we can practise our profession together, and I can carry out all my plans. But first - first - he wants me to - marry him!"

"Who?"

"Don't you know? Dr. Mulbridge!"

"That - I beg your pardon. I've no right to call him names." The young fellow halted, and looked at her downcast face. "Well, do you want me to tell you to take him? That is too much. I didn't know you were cruel."

"You make me cruel! You leave me to be cruel!"

"I leave you to be cruel?"

"Oh, don't play upon my words, if you won't ask me what I answered!"

"How can I ask that? I have no right to know."

"But you shall know!" she cried. "I told him that I had no plans. I have given them all up because - because I'm too weak for them, and because I abhor him, and because - But it wasn't enough. He would not take what I said for answer, and he is coming again for an answer."

"Coming again?"

"Yes. He is a man who believes that women may change, for reason or no reason; and" -

"You - you mean to take him when he comes back?" gasped the young man.

"Never! Not if he came a thousand times!"

"Then what is it you want me to advise you about?" he faltered.

"Nothing!" she answered, with freezing hauteur. She suddenly put up her arms across her eyes, with the beautiful, artless action of a shame-smitten child, and left her young figure in bewildering relief. "Oh, don't you see that I love you?"

"Couldn't you understand, - couldn't you see what I meant?" she asked again that night, as they lost themselves on the long stretch of the moonlit beach. With his arm close about that lovely shape they would have seemed but one person to the inattentive observer, as they paced along in the white splendor.

"I couldn't risk anything. I had spoken, once for all. I always thought that for a man to offer himself twice was indelicate and unfair. I could never have done it."

"That's very sweet in you," she said; and perhaps she would have praised in the same terms the precisely opposite sentiment. "It's some comfort," she added, with a deep-fetched sigh, "to think I had to speak."

He laughed. "You didn't find it so easy to make love!"

"Oh, NOTHING is easy that men have to do!" she answered, with passionate earnestness.

There are moments of extreme concession, of magnanimous admission, that come but once in a lifetime.

XII

Dr. Mulbridge did not wait for the time he had fixed for his return. He may have judged that her tendency against him would strengthen by delay, or he may have yielded to his own impatience in coming the next day. He asked for Grace with his wonted abruptness, and waited for her coming in the little parlor of the hotel, walking up and down the floor, with his shaggy head bent forward, and his big hands clasped behind him.

As she hovered at the door before entering, she could watch him while he walked the whole room's length away, and she felt a pang at sight of him. If she could have believed that he loved her, she could not have faced him, but must have turned and run away; and even as it was she grieved for him. Such a man would not have made up his mind to this step without a deep motive, if not a deep feeling. Her heart had been softened so that she could not think of frustrating his ambition, if it were no better than that, without pity. One man had made her feel very kindly toward all other men; she wished in the tender confusion of the moment that she need not reject her importunate suitor, whose importunity even she could not resent.

He caught sight of her as soon as he made his turn at the end of the room, and with a quick "Ah, Ah!" he hastened to meet her, with the smile in which there was certainly something attractive. "You see I've come back a day sooner than I promised. I haven't the sort of turnout you've been used to, but I want you to drive with me." "I can't drive with you, Dr. Mulbridge," she faltered.

"Well, walk, then. I should prefer to walk."

"You must excuse me," she answered, and remained standing before him.

"Sit down," he bade her, and pushed up a chair towards her. His audacity, if it had been a finer courage, would have been splendid, and as it was she helplessly obeyed him, as if she were his patient, and must do so. "If I were superstitious I should say that you receive me ominously," he said, fixing his gray eyes keenly upon her.

"I do!" she forced herself to reply. "I wish you had not come."

"That's explicit, at any rate. Have you thought it over?"

"No; I had no need to do that, I had fully resolved when I spoke yesterday. Dr. Mulbridge, why didn't you spare me this? It's unkind of you to insist, after what I said. You know that I must hate to repeat it. I do value you so highly in some ways that I blame you for obliging me to hurt you - if it does hurt - by telling you again that I don't love you."

He drew in a long breath, and set his teeth hard upon his lip. "You may depend upon its hurting," he said, "but I was glad to risk the pain, whatever it was, for the chance of getting you to reconsider. I presume I'm not the conventional wooer. I'm too old for it, and I'm too blunt and plain a man. I've been thirty-five years making up my mind to ask you to marry me. You're the first woman, and you shall be the last. You couldn't suppose I was going to give you up for one no?"

"You had better."

"Not for twenty! I can understand very well how you never thought of me in this way; but there's no reason why you shouldn't. Come, it's a matter that we can reason about, like anything else."

"No. I told you, it's something we can't reason about. Or yes, it is. I will reason with you. You say that you love me?"

"Yes."

"If you didn't love me, you wouldn't ask me to marry you?"

"No."

"Then how can you expect me to marry you without loving you?"

"I don't. All that I ask is that you won't refuse me. I know that you can love me."

"No, no, never!"

"And I only want you to take time to try."

"I don't wish to try. If you persist, I must leave the room. We had better part. I was foolish to see you. But I thought - I was sorry - I hoped to make it less unkind to you."

"In spite of yourself, you were relenting."

"Not at all!"

"But if you pitied me, you did care for me a little?"

"You know that I had the highest respect for you as a physician. I tell you that you were my ideal in that way, and I will tell you that if" - she stopped, and he continued for her.

"If you had not resolved to give it up, you might have done what I asked."

"I did not say that," she answered indignantly.

"But why do you give it up?"

"Because I am not equal to it."

"How do you know it? Who told you?"

"You have told me, - by every look and act of yours, - and I'm grateful to you for it."

"And if I told you now by word that you were fit for it."

"I shouldn't believe you."

"You wouldn't believe my word?" She did not answer. "I see," he said presently, "that you doubt me somehow as a man. What is it you think of me?"

"You wouldn't like to know."

"Oh, yes, I should."

"Well, I will tell you. I think you are a tyrant, and that you want a slave, not a wife. You wish to be obeyed. You despise women. I don't mean their minds, - they're despicable enough, in most cases, as men's are, - but their nature."

"This is news to me," he said, laughing. "I never knew that I despised women's nature."

"It's true, whether you knew it or not."

"Do I despise you?"

"You would, if you saw that I was afraid of you: Oh, why do you force me to say such things? Why don't you spare me - spare yourself?"

"In this cause I couldn't spare myself. I can't bear to give you up! I'm what I am, whatever you say; but with you, I could be whatever you would. I could show you that you are wrong if you gave me the chance. I know that I could make you happy. Listen to me a moment."

"It's useless."

"No! If you have taken the trouble to read me in this way, there must have been a time when you might have cared."

"There never was any such time. I read you from the first."

"I will go away," he said, after a pause, in which she had risen, and began a retreat towards the door. "But I will not - I cannot - give you up. I will see you again."

"No, sir. You shall not see me again. I will not submit to it. I will not be persecuted." She was trembling, and she knew that he saw her tremor.

"Well," he said, with a smile that recognized her trepidation, "I will not persecute you. I'll renounce these pretensions. But I'll ask you to see me once more, as a friend, - an acquaintance."

"I will not see you again."

"You are rather hard with me, I think," he urged gently. "I don't think I'm playing the tyrant with you now."

"You are, - the baffled tyrant."

"But if I promised not to offend again, why should you deny me your acquaintance?"

"Because I don't believe you." She was getting nearer the door, and as she put her hand behind her and touched the knob, the wild terror she had felt, lest he should reach it first and prevent her escape, left her. "You are treating me like a child that doesn't know its own mind, or has none to know. You are laughing at me - playing with me; you have shown me that you despise me."

He actually laughed. "Well, you've shown that you are not afraid of me. Why are you not afraid?"

"Because," she answered, and she dealt the blow now without pity, "I'm engaged, - engaged to Mr. Libby!" She whirled about and vanished through the door, ashamed, indignant, fearing that if she had not fled, he would somehow have found means to make his will prevail even yet.

He stood, stupefied, looking at the closed door, and he made a turn or two about the room before he summoned intelligence to quit it. When death itself comes, the sense of continuance is not at once broken in the survivors. In these moral deaths, which men survive in their own lives, there is no immediate consciousness of an end. For a while, habit and the automatic tendency of desire carry them on.

He drove back to Corbitant perched on the rickety seat of his rattling open buggy, and bowed forward as his wont was, his rounded shoulders bringing his chin well over the dashboard. As he passed down the long sandy street, toward the corner where his own house stood, the brooding group of loafers, waiting in Hackett's store for the distribution of the mail, watched him through the open door, and from under the boughs of the weatherbeaten poplar before it. Hackett had been cutting a pound of cheese out of the thick yellow disk before him, for the Widow Holman, and he stared at the street after Mulbridge passed, as if his mental eye had halted him there for the public consideration, while he leaned over the counter, and held by the point the long knife with which he had cut the cheese.

"I see some the folks from over to Jocelyn's, yist'd'y," he said, in a spasm of sharp, crackling speech, "and they seemed to think 't Mis' Mulbridge'd got to step round pretty spry 'f she

William Dean Howells

didn't want another the same name in the house with her."

A long silence followed, in which no one changed in any wise the posture in which he found himself when Hackett began to speak. Cap'n George Wray, tilted back against the wall in his chair, continued to stare at the store-keeper; Cap'n Jabez Wray, did not look up from whittling the chair between his legs; their cousin, Cap'n Wray Storrell, seated on a nailkeg near the stove, went on fretting the rust on the pipe with the end of a stiff, cast-off envelope; two other captains, more or less akin to them, continued their game of checkers; the Widow Seth Wray's boy rested immovable, with his chin and hand on the counter, where he had been trying since the Widow Holman went out to catch Hackett's eye and buy a corn-ball. Old Cap'n Billy Wray was the first to break the spell. He took his cigar from his mouth, and held it between his shaking thumb and forefinger, while he pursed his lips for speech. "Jabez," he said, "did Cap'n Sam'l git that coalier?"

"No," answered the whittler, cutting deeper into his chair, "she didn't signal for him till she got into the channel, and then he'd got a couple o' passengers for Leyden; and Cap'n Jim brought her up."

"I don't know," said Cap'n Billy, with a stiff yet tremulous reference of himself to the storekeeper, "as spryness would help her, as long as he took the notion. I guess he's master of his own ship. Who's he going to marry? The grahs-widow got well enough?"

"No. As I understand," crackled the store-keeper, "her husband's turned up. Folks over there seem to think't he's got his eye on the other doctor."

"Going to marry with her, hey? Well, if either of 'em gets sick they won't have to go far for advice, and they won't have any doctor's bills to pay. Still, I shouldn't ha' picked out just that kind of a wife for him."

"As I understand," the storekeeper began; but here he caught sight of Widow Seth Wray's boy, and asked, "What's wanted, Bub? Corn-ball?" and turning to take that sweetmeat from the shelf behind him he added the rest in the mouth of the hollowly reverberating jar, "She's got prop'ty."

"Well, I never knew a Mulbridge yet 't objected to prop'ty, - especially, other folks's."

"Barlow he's tellin' round that she's very fine appearin'." He handed the corn-ball to Widow Seth Wray's boy, who went noiselessly out on his bare feet.

Cap'n Billy drew several long breaths. When another man might have been supposed to have dismissed the subject he said, "Well, I never knew a Mulbridge that objected to good looks in women folks. They've all married hahnsome wives, ever since the old gentleman set 'em the example with his second one. They got their own looks from the first. Well," he added, "I hope she's a tough one. She's got either to bend or to break."

"They say," said Cap'n George Wray, like one rising from the dead to say it, so dumb and motionless had he been till now, "that Mis' Mulbridge was too much for the old doctor."

"I don't know about that," Cap'n Billy replied, "but I guess her son's too much for her: she's only Gardiner, and he's Gardiner and Mulbridge both."

No one changed countenance, but a sense of Cap'n Billy's wit sparely yet satisfyingly glimmered from the eyes of Cap'n George and the storekeeper, and Cap'n Jabez closed his knife with a snap and looked up. "Perhaps," he suggested, "she's seen enough of him to know beforehand that there would be too much of him."

"I never rightly understood," said Hackett, "just what it was about him, there in the army - coming out a year beforehand,

William Dean Howells

that way."

"I guess you never will, - from him," said Cap'n Jabez.

"Laziness, I guess, - too much work," said old Cap'n Billy. "What he wants is a wife with money. There ain't a better doctor anywhere. I've heard 't up to Boston, where he got his manifest, they thought everything of him. He's smart enough, but he's lazy, and he always was lazy, and harder'n a nut. He's a curious mixtur'. 'N' I guess he's been on the lookout for somethin' of this kind ever sence he begun practising among the summer boarders. Guess he's had an eye out."

"They say he's poplar among 'em," observed the storekeeper thoughtfully.

"He's been pooty p'tic'lar, or they have," said Cap'n Jabez.

"Well, most on 'em's married women," Hackett urged. "It's astonishin' how they do come off and leave their husbands, the whole summer long. They say they're all out o' health, though."

"I wonder," said old Cap'n Billy, "if them coaliers is goin' to make a settled thing of haulin' inside before they signal a pilot."

"I know one thing," answered Cap'n Jabez, "that if any coalier signals me in the channel, I'll see her in hell first" He slipped his smooth, warm knife into his pocket, and walked out of the store amid a general silence.

"He's consid'ble worked up, about them coaliers," said old Cap'n Billy. "I don't know as I've heard Jabez swear before - not since he was mate of the Gallatin. He used to swear then, consid'able."

"Them coaliers is enough to make any one swear," said Cap'n George. "If it's any ways fair weather they won't take you outside, and they cut you down from twenty-five dollars to two dollars if they take you inside."

Old Cap'n Billy did not answer before he had breathed awhile, and then, having tried his cigar and found it out, he scraped a match on his coat-sleeve. He looked at the flame while it burned from blue to yellow. "Well, I guess if anybody's been p'tic'lar, it's been him. There ain't any doubt but what he's got a takin' way with the women. They like him. He's masterful, and he ain't a fool, and women most gen'ly like a man that ain't a fool. I guess if he's got his eye on the girl's prop'ty, she'll have to come along. He'd begin by havin' his own way about her answer; he'd hang on till she said Yes, if she didn't say it first-off; and he'd keep on as he'd begun. I guess if he wants her it's a match." And Cap'n Billy threw his own into the square box of tobacco-stained sawdust under the stove.

Mrs. Maynard fully shared the opinion which rocked Dr. Mulbridge's defeat with a belief in his invincible will. When it became necessary, in the course of events which made Grace and Libby resolve upon a short engagement, to tell her that they were going to be married, she expressed a frank astonishment. "Walter Libby!" she cried. "Well, I am surprised. When I was talking to you the other day about getting married, of course I supposed it was going to be Dr. Mulbridge. I didn't want you to marry him, but I thought you were going to."

"And why," demanded Grace, with mounting sensation, "did you think that?"

"Oh, I thought you would have to."

"Have to?"

"Oh, you have such a weak will. Or I always thought you had. But perhaps it's only a weak will with other women. I don't know! But Walter Libby! I knew he was perfectly gone upon you, and I told you so at the beginning; but I never dreamt of your caring for him. Why, it seems too ridiculous."

"Indeed! I'm glad that it amuses you."

"Oh no, you're not, Grace. But you know what I mean. He seems so much younger."

"Younger? He's half a year older than I am."

"I didn't say he was younger. But you're so very grave and he's so very light. Well, I always told Walter Libby I should get him a wife, but you were the last person I should have thought of. What's going to become of all your high purposes? You can't do anything with them when you're married! But you won't have any occasion for them, that's one comfort."

"It's not my idea of marriage that any high purpose will be lost in it."

"Oh, it isn't anybody's, before they get married. I had such high purposes I couldn't rest. I felt like hiring a hall, as George says, all the time. Walter Libby isn't going to let you practise, is he? You mustn't let him! I know he'd be willing to do anything you said, but a husband ought to be something more than a mere & Co."

Grace laughed at the impudent cynicism of all this, for she was too happy to be vexed with any one just then. "I'm glad you've come to think so well of husbands' rights at last, Louise," she said.

Mrs. Maynard took the little puncture in good part. "Oh, yes, George and I have had a good deal of light let in on us. I don't suppose my character was much changed outwardly in my sickness," she suggested.

"It was not," answered Grace warmly. "It was intensified, that was all."

Mrs. Maynard laughed in her turn, with real enjoyment of the conception. "Well, I wasn't going to let on, unless it came to the worst; I didn't say much, but I kept up an awful thinking. It would have been easy enough to get a divorce, and George wouldn't have opposed it; but I looked at it in this way: that the divorce wouldn't have put us back where we were, anyway, as I had supposed it would. We had broken into each other's lives, and we couldn't get out again, with all the divorces under the sun. That's the worst of getting married: you break into each other's lives. You said something like it to me, that day when you came back from your sail with Walter Libby. And I just concluded that there couldn't be any trial that wouldn't be a great deal easier to bear than getting rid of all your trials; and I just made up my mind that if any divorce was to be got, George Maynard might get it himself; a temporary separation was bad enough for me, and I told him so, about the first words I could speak. And we're going to try the new departure on that platform. We don't either of us suspect we can have things perfectly smooth, but we've agreed to rough it together when we can't. We've found out that we can't marry and then become single, any more than we could die and come to life again. And don't you forget it, Grace! You don't half know yourself, now. You know what you have been; but getting married lets loose all your possibilities. You don't know what a temper you've got, nor how badly you can behave - how much like a naughty, good-for-nothing little girl; for a husband and wife are just two children together: that's what makes the sweetness of it, and that's what makes the dreadfulness. Oh, you'll have need of all your good principles, I can tell you, and if you've a mind to do anything practical in the way of high purposes, I reckon there'll be use for them all."

Another lady who was astonished at Grace's choice was more incurably disappointed and more grieved for the waste of those noble aims with which her worshipping fancy had endowed the girl even more richly than her own ambition. It was Grace's wish to pass a year in Europe before her husband should settle down in charge of his mills; and their engagement, marriage, and departure followed so swiftly upon one another, that Miss Gleason would have had no opportunity to proffer remonstrance or advice. She could only account for

Grace's course on the theory that Dr. Mulbridge had failed to offer himself; but this explained her failure to marry him, without explaining her marriage with Mr. Libby. That remained for some time a mystery, for Miss Gleason firmly refused to believe that such a girl could be in love with a man so much her inferior: the conception disgraced not only her idol, but cast shame upon all other women, whose course in such matters is notoriously governed by motives of the highest sagacity and judgment.

Mrs. Breen hesitated between the duty of accompanying the young couple on their European travels, and that of going to the village where Libby's mills were situated, - in southern New Hampshire. She was not strongly urged to a decision by her children, and she finally chose the latter course. The mill property had been a long time abandoned before Libby's father bought it, and put it in a repair which he did not hasten to extend to the village. This had remained in a sort of picturesque neglect, which harmonized with the scenery of the wild little valley where it nestled; and Mrs. Breen found, upon the vigorous inquiry which she set on foot, that the operatives were deplorably destitute of culture and drainage. She at once devoted herself to the establishment of a circulating library and an enlightened system of cess-pools, to such an effect of ingratitude in her beneficiaries that she was quite ready to remand them to their former squalor when her son-in-law returned. But he found her work all so good that he mediated between her and the inhabitants, and adopted it with a hearty appreciation that went far to console her, and finally popularized it. In fact, he entered into the spirit of all practical reforms with an energy and intelligence that quite reconciled her to him. It was rather with Grace than with him that she had fault to find. She believed that the girl had returned from Europe materialized and corrupted; and she regarded the souvenirs of travel with which the house was filled as so many tokens of moral decay. It is undeniable that Grace seemed for a time, to have softened to, a certain degree of self-indulgence. During the brief opera season the first winter after her return, she spent a week in Boston; she often came to the city, and went to the theatres and the exhibitions of pictures. It was for some time Miss Gleason's opinion that these escapades were the struggles of a magnanimous nature, unequally mated, to forget itself. When they met she indulged the habit of regarding Mrs. Libby with eyes of latent pity, till one day she heard something that gave her more relief than she could ever have hoped for. This was the fact, perfectly ascertained by some summer sojourners in the neighborhood; that Mrs. Libby was turning her professional training to account by treating the sick children among her husband's operatives.

In the fall Miss Gleason saw her heroine at an exhibition of pictures. She rushed across the main hall of the Museum to greet her. "Congratulate you!" she deeply whispered, "on realizing your dream! Now you are happy, now you can be at peace!"

"Happy? At peace?"

"In the good work you have taken up. Oh, nothing, under Gawd, is lost!" she exclaimed, getting ready to run away, and speaking with her face turned over her shoulder towards Mrs. Libby.

"Dream? Good work? What do you mean?"

"Those factory children!"

"Oh!" said Mrs. Libby coldly, "that was my husband's idea."

"Your husband's!" cried Miss Gleason, facing about again, and trying to let a whole history of suddenly relieved anxiety speak in her eyes. "How happy you make me! Do let me thank you!"

In the effort to shake hands with Mrs. Libby she knocked the catalogue out of her hold, and vanished in the crowd without knowing it. Some gentleman picked it up, and gave it to her again, with a bow of burlesque devotion.

Mrs. Libby flushed tenderly. "I might have known it would be you, Walter. Where did you spring from?"

"I've been here ever since you came."

"What in the world doing?"

"Oh, enjoying myself."

"Looking at the pictures?"

"Watching you walk round:'

"I thought you couldn't be enjoying the pictures," she said simply. "I'm not."

She was not happy, indeed, in any of the aesthetic dissipations into which she had plunged, and it was doubtless from a shrewder knowledge of her nature than she had herself that her husband had proposed this active usefulness, which she once intended under such different conditions. At the end of the ends she was a Puritan; belated, misdated, if the reader will, and cast upon good works for the consolation which the Puritans formerly found in a creed. Riches and ease were sinful to her, and somehow to be atoned for; and she had no real love for anything that was not of an immediate humane and spiritual effect. Under the shelter of her husband's name the benevolent use of her skill was no queerer than the charity to which many ladies devote themselves; though they are neither of them people to have felt the anguish which comes from the fear of what other people will think. They go their way in life, and are probably not disturbed by any misgivings concerning them. It is thought, on one hand, that he is a man of excellent head, and of a heart so generous that his deference to her in certain matters is part of the devoted flattery which would spoil any other woman, but that she consults his judgment in every action of her life, and trusts his sense with the same completeness that she trusts his love. On the other hand, when it is felt that she ought to have done for the sake of woman what she could not do for herself, she is regarded as sacrificed in her marriage. If, it is feared, she is not infatuated with her husband, she is in a disgraceful subjection, without the hope of better or higher things. If she had children, they might be a compensation and refuge for her; in that case, to be sure, she must be cut off from her present resource in caring for the children of others; though the conditions under which she now exercises her skill certainly amount to begging the whole question of woman's fitness for the career she had chosen.

Both parties to this contention are, strange to say, ladies. If it has not been made clear from the events and characters of the foregoing history which opinion is right, I am unable to decide. It is well, perhaps, not to be too explicitly in the confidence of one's heroine. After her marriage perhaps it is not even decorous.

William Dean Howells

Choose from Thousands of 1stWorldLibrary Classics By

A. M. Barnard
Ada Leverson
Adolphus William Ward
Aesop
Agatha Christie
Alexander Aaronsohn
Alexander Kielland
Alexandre Dumas
Alfred Gatty
Alfred Ollivant
Alice Duer Miller
Alice Turner Curtis
Alice Dunbar
Allen Chapman
Ambrose Bierce
Amelia E. Barr
Amory H. Bradford
Andrew Lang
Andrew McFarland Davis
Andy Adams
Anna Alice Chapin
Anna Sewell
Annie Besant
Annie Hamilton Donnell
Annie Payson Call
Annie Roe Carr
Annonaymous
Anton Chekhov
Arnold Bennett
Arthur Conan Doyle
Arthur M. Winfield
Arthur Ransome
Arthur Schnitzler
Atticus
B.H. Baden-Powell
B. M. Bower
B. C. Chatterjee
Baroness Emmuska Orczy
Baroness Orczy
Basil King
Bayard Taylor
Ben Macomber
Bertha Muzzy Bower
Bjornstjerne Bjornson
Booth Tarkington
Boyd Cable
Bram Stoker
C. Collodi
C. E. Orr

C. M. Ingleby
Carolyn Wells
Catherine Parr Traill
Charles A. Eastman
Charles Amory Beach
Charles Dickens
Charles Dudley Warner
Charles Farrar Browne
Charles Ives
Charles Kingsley
Charles Klein
Charles Hanson Towne
Charles Lathrop Pack
Charles Romyn Dake
Charles Whibley
Charles Willing Beale
Charlotte M. Braeme
Charlotte M. Yonge
Charlotte Perkins Stetson
Clair W. Hayes
Clarence Day Jr.
Clarence E. Mulford
Clemence Housman
Confucius
Coningsby Dawson
Cornelis DeWitt Wilcox
Cyril Burleigh
D. H. Lawrence
Daniel Defoe
David Garnett
Dinah Craik
Don Carlos Janes
Donald Keyhoe
Dorothy Kilner
Dougan Clark
Douglas Fairbanks
E. Nesbit
E.P.Roe
E. Phillips Oppenheim
Earl Barnes
Edgar Rice Burroughs
Edith Van Dyne
Edith Wharton
Edward Everett Hale
Edward J. O'Biren
Edward S. Ellis
Edwin L. Arnold
Eleanor Atkins
Eliot Gregory

Elizabeth Gaskell
Elizabeth McCracken
Elizabeth Von Arnim
Ellem Key
Emerson Hough
Emilie F. Carlen
Emily Dickinson
Enid Bagnold
Enilor Macartney Lane
Erasmus W. Jones
Ernie Howard Pie
Ethel May Dell
Ethel Turner
Ethel Watts Mumford
Eugenie Foa
Eugene Wood
Eustace Hale Ball
Evelyn Everett-green
Everard Cotes
F. H. Cheley
F. J. Cross
F. Marion Crawford
Federick Austin Ogg
Ferdinand Ossendowski
Francis Bacon
Francis Darwin
Frances Hodgson Burnett
Frances Parkinson Keyes
Frank Gee Patchin
Frank Harris
Frank Jewett Mather
Frank L. Packard
Frank V. Webster
Frederic Stewart Isham
Frederick Trevor Hill
Frederick Winslow Taylor
Friedrich Kerst
Friedrich Nietzsche
Fyodor Dostoyevsky
G.A. Henty
G.K. Chesterton
Gabrielle E. Jackson
Garrett P. Serviss
Gaston Leroux
George A. Warren
George Ade
Geroge Bernard Shaw
George Durston
George Ebers

George Eliot
George Gissing
George MacDonald
George Meredith
George Orwell
George Sylvester Viereck
George Tucker
George W. Cable
George Wharton James
Gertrude Atherton
Gordon Casserly
Grace E. King
Grace Gallatin
Grace Greenwood
Grant Allen
Guillermo A. Sherwell
Gulielma Zollinger
Gustav Flaubert
H. A. Cody
H. B. Irving
H.C. Bailey
H. G. Wells
H. H. Munro
H. Irving Hancock
H. Rider Haggard
H. W. C. Davis
Haldeman Julius
Hall Caine
Hamilton Wright Mabie
Hans Christian Andersen
Harold Avery
Harold McGrath
Harriet Beecher Stowe
Harry Castlemon
Harry Coghill
Harry Houidini
Hayden Carruth
Helent Hunt Jackson
Helen Nicolay
Hendrik Conscience
Hendy David Thoreau
Henri Barbusse
Henrik Ibsen
Henry Adams
Henry Ford
Henry Frost
Henry James
Henry Jones Ford
Henry Seton Merriman
Henry W Longfellow
Herbert A. Giles

Herbert Carter
Herbert N. Casson
Herman Hesse
Hildegard G. Frey
Homer
Honore De Balzac
Horace B. Day
Horace Walpole
Horatio Alger Jr.
Howard Pyle
Howard R. Garis
Hugh Lofting
Hugh Walpole
Humphry Ward
Ian Maclaren
Inez Haynes Gillmore
Irving Bacheller
Isabel Hornibrook
Israel Abrahams
Ivan Turgenev
J.G.Austin
J. Henri Fabre
J. M. Barrie
J. Macdonald Oxley
J. S. Fletcher
J. S. Knowles
J. Storer Clouston
Jack London
Jacob Abbott
James Allen
James Andrews
James Baldwin
James Branch Cabell
James DeMille
James Joyce
James Lane Allen
James Lane Allen
James Oliver Curwood
James Oppenheim
James Otis
James R. Driscoll
Jane Austen
Jane L. Stewart
Janet Aldridge
Jens Peter Jacobsen
Jerome K. Jerome
John Burroughs
John Cournos
John F. Kennedy
John Gay
John Glasworthy

John Habberton
John Joy Bell
John Kendrick Bangs
John Milton
John Philip Sousa
Jonas Lauritz Idemil Lie
Jonathan Swift
Joseph A. Altsheler
Joseph Carey
Joseph Conrad
Joseph E. Badger Jr
Joseph Hergesheimer
Joseph Jacobs
Jules Vernes
Julian Hawthrone
Julie A Lippmann
Justin Huntly McCarthy
Kakuzo Okakura
Kenneth Grahame
Kenneth McGaffey
Kate Langley Bosher
Kate Langley Bosher
Katherine Cecil Thurston
Katherine Stokes
L. A. Abbot
L. T. Meade
L. Frank Baum
Latta Griswold
Laura Dent Crane
Laura Lee Hope
Laurence Housman
Lawrence Beasley
Leo Tolstoy
Leonid Andreyev
Lewis Carroll
Lewis Sperry Chafer
Lilian Bell
Lloyd Osbourne
Louis Hughes
Louis Tracy
Louisa May Alcott
Lucy Fitch Perkins
Lucy Maud Montgomery
Luther Benson
Lydia Miller Middleton
Lyndon Orr
M. Corvus
M. H. Adams
Margaret E. Sangster
Margret Howth
Margaret Vandercook

Margret Penrose
Maria Edgeworth
Maria Thompson Daviess
Mariano Azuela
Marion Polk Angellotti
Mark Overton
Mark Twain
Mary Austin
Mary Catherine Crowley
Mary Cole
Mary Hastings Bradley
Mary Roberts Rinehart
Mary Rowlandson
M. Wollstonecraft Shelley
Maud Lindsay
Max Beerbohm
Myra Kelly
Nathaniel Hawthrone
Nicolo Machiavelli
O. F. Walton
Oscar Wilde
Owen Johnson
P.G. Wodehouse
Paul and Mabel Thorne
Paul G. Tomlinson
Paul Severing
Percy Brebner
Peter B. Kyne
Plato
R. Derby Holmes
R. L. Stevenson
R. S. Ball
Rabindranath Tagore
Rahul Alvares
Ralph Bonehill
Ralph Henry Barbour
Ralph Victor
Ralph Waldo Emmerson
Rene Descartes
Rex Beach

Rex E. Beach
Richard Harding Davis
Richard Jefferies
Richard Le Gallienne
Robert Barr
Robert Frost
Robert Gordon Anderson
Robert L. Drake
Robert Lansing
Robert Lynd
Robert Michael Ballantyne
Robert W. Chambers
Rosa Nouchette Carey
Rudyard Kipling
Samuel B. Allison
Samuel Hopkins Adams
Sarah Bernhardt
Sarah C. Hallowell
Selma Lagerlof
Sherwood Anderson
Sigmund Freud
Standish O'Grady
Stanley Weyman
Stella Benson
Stella M. Francis
Stephen Crane
Stewart Edward White
Stijn Streuvels
Swami Abhedananda
Swami Parmananda
T. S. Ackland
T. S. Arthur
The Princess Der Ling
Thomas A. Janvier
Thomas A Kempis
Thomas Anderton
Thomas Bailey Aldrich
Thomas Bulfinch
Thomas De Quincey
Thomas Dixon

Thomas H. Huxley
Thomas Hardy
Thomas More
Thornton W. Burgess
U. S. Grant
Valentine Williams
Various Authors
Vaughan Kester
Victor Appleton
Victoria Cross
Virginia Woolf
Wadsworth Camp
Walter Camp
Walter Scott
Washington Irving
Wilbur Lawton
Wilkie Collins
Willa Cather
Willard F. Baker
William Dean Howells
William le Queux
W. Makepeace Thackeray
William W. Walter
William Shakespeare
Winston Churchill
Yei Theodora Ozaki
Yogi Ramacharaka
Young E. Allison
Zane Grey